# Prophets And Deliverance

Written By

JUDITH JOHN

Copyright © 2020 Judith John

All rights reserved.

ISBN: 978-0-578-87026-7

## Table of Contents

Dedication ....................................................................................... vi

Thank You ..................................................................................... vii

Forward ............................................................................................ 2

From the Author ............................................................................. 8

    Prophetic and Warning Dream .................................................. 13

Chapter 1 The Soul ....................................................................... 18

    Defining the Soul ........................................................................ 19

    The Making of Humanity .......................................................... 20

    The Physical Meets the Spiritual .............................................. 21

    In the Beginning ......................................................................... 22

    Authentic Dominion .................................................................. 23

    Souly Overthrow the Legislation in Effect ............................. 27

    Where It All Began .................................................................... 29

    Faith and the Mind .................................................................... 31

Chapter 2 Sinful Doorways ........................................................ 33

    Doorways to Other Influences ................................................. 34

    Change in Leadership ............................................................... 36

    Leadership & Identity ............................................................... 35

Idolatry and the Church ............................................................. 39

Satan's Agenda ........................................................................... 41

Here's Your Symbol .................................................................... 41

**Chapter 3 Deliverance ............................................................. 46**

Part 1 ........................................................................................... 46

    Light and Lesser Light ............................................................ 51

    Promissory Note of Freedom .................................................. 52

    Tools: The Spirit of Prophecy and Atmospheres ................... 53

    Deliverance for the Prophet First ........................................... 55

**Chapter 4 Deliverance ............................................................. 57**

PART 2 ........................................................................................ 57

    Systems and Cycles ................................................................. 57

    Deliverance: New Birth ........................................................... 65

    Fear and Deliverance .............................................................. 66

    Deliverance: Tolerance and Sin .............................................. 68

    Having A Consistent Mentality .............................................. 70

    Problematic Prophets/Ministers ............................................. 71

**Chapter 5 Symbolism, The Prophetic & Prophets ................ 73**

    Symbolism: Dreams & Visions ............................................... 75

The Prophetic ...................................................................77

Prophets .........................................................................79

## Chapter 6 Soul of the Prophet ..................................82

Soul of the Prophet .......................................................82

## Chapter 7 Abuse Of Power ........................................86

Part 1 ..............................................................................86

    Honor vs. False Honor ............................................86

    Godly Honor ............................................................88

    What is In Identity ...................................................88

    False Honor and Theft ............................................90

    Identity Theft ...........................................................91

    Navigate Through ...................................................92

    Co-dependency ........................................................93

    Soul Ties ....................................................................95

    Abuse of Power and Language ..............................97

    Abuse of Power and Trauma Bonding ................98

## Chapter 8 Abuse of Power ........................................102

Part 2 ............................................................................102

    Ways to Prevent Trauma Bonding .....................102

Proof of Identity ................................................................... 104

Other Abuses of Power ........................................................ 106

Pride Attempts to Hides Things ........................................... 108

**Chapter 9 Communication Realm** ............................................... **111**

Communication: Actions and Behaviors ............................... 118

Communication: Worship ..................................................... 120

The Mechanics of Prayer ....................................................... 122

**Chapter 10 Glory Carriers** ........................................................... **125**

New Era Where People Are In Training ............................... 131

**The END** ....................................................................................... **137**

**About the Author** ........................................................................ **138**

**Citations** ....................................................................................... **140**

## Dedication

To dedicate this book to you is my honor. The truth is there is no other qualified contender with whom I hold in higher esteem, Sir. Let this mark the beginning of many endeavors we complete together to advance the Matthew 6:10 edict. Let thy kingdom come, Elohim. To you, my Lord!

## Thank You

Thank you for always supporting me. Thank God for your brave, loyal heart, and I pray blessings and supernatural wisdom for you, my brother, and your children. I am thankful for our connection Mrs. Cassandra Georges.

Thank you, Minister Andrea Rackley, for answering the phone when I needed a medical professional's ear and opinion. Your insight gave me another perspective about the ending of this book. May God continue to prosper you and your family with health and wholeness.

# FORWARD

If there has ever been a need to restore and heal the soul, the time is now. We live in a time in history where we face some of the most complex crises of our time. It has been said that difficulties, challenges, and controversy serve as a barometer to measure a person's character. I would take this notion further by saying that these things ultimately reveal the need for soul work that leads to freedom and deliverance. Isaiah 60:2 declares, "For behold, the darkness shall cover the earth, and deep darkness the people; But the LORD will arise over you, And His glory will be seen upon you"; we are in these days where it is seemingly impossible to live through.

The year 2020 ushered the world into a brand-new era. As fear and uncertainty gripped the hearts of mankind, we witnessed a devastating time of loss and pain. The world as we once knew it shifted, and what was familiar and comfortable no longer brought us joy and happiness. The intensified warfare left many people lost, confused, and hopeless, looking for a way to escape and recover from the battles both in the realm of the spirit and in the natural. If these truths bear witness to your spirit, the book you are holding is an end-time prophetic war weapon to help you recover your soul.

Prophets are God's divine projectiles assigned to dismantle darkness and legislate the kingdom's affairs on the earth. God is calling for Holy prophets who will die to themselves and confront the darkness within to effectively dismantle, overturn and disallow darkness without. Deliverance is intentional. If prophets are to arise to repair fragmented souls, they must first exercise dominion over their own souls. When this happens, engaging in spiritual reconnaissance to recover and restore fractured and bruised souls become easy.

I am so proud of my spiritual daughter, Prophet Judith John. She has done her due diligence to pen keys to release captives from their captivity. A profound researcher and a knowledgeable teacher about prophetic deliverance, she is a frontline warrior and my chief intercessor. Prophets and Deliverance is a necessary tool for every 5-fold leader. It will take you on a soul-searching journey of healing, deliverance, and breakthrough to empower you to step into your moment of dominance and authority. I believe this book is the birthing of the process she has lived. T. Austin Sparks said, "As a prophet, people do not come to hear you speak, but they come to see who you are." In other words, the person embodies the message they speak.

May your cry for help and breakthrough be answered through every page you read. May God unlock the mind of your soul and free you from all falsehoods, lies, blockages, and bondages. Finally, may you understand that you were created for what you are about to live NOW.

Apostle Cynthia Thompson
Jesus People Proclaim International Church
The Prophetic Institute
Author of The Power of a Prophetic Mindset

# FORWARD

The prophet's office was founded before time and was released in time to display the purity, potency, and power housed within the mind of God. From now until Messiah returns, there will always be a need for deliverance and the anointed release of the voiceprint of Elohim in the earth. As one who has been given oversight as chief over prophets and prophetic types, I understand the critical need for training and governance in the prophetic realm. After many years of wild and ungoverned prophetic operations, God is raising up a fleet of prophetic footmen who will lay a foundation to establish prophetic character, acumen, and understanding. Those who have prayed and sought the Father for a prophetic guidepost that would break up, demystify, and teach prophets how to overcome issues of the soul; you do not have to look any further. The book you are holding was not birthed of a theory, but rather it was inwrought in Prophet Judith through her life experiences. As you read each chapter, you will see that she has exercised due diligence in constructing a manuscript representative of the agency of the prophetic. The revelation and truth contained in this book are transformational and will prepare budding prophets, institutional prophets, company prophets, chief prophets how to be whole in their service to God. I endorse this book as well as this end-time prophetic reformer whom I personally know defends the cause of Christ. If you are a leader, you can feel confident knowing that you are holding the key to your next. Judith John's Prophet's and Deliverance is a must-have for anyone who thinks that they measure somewhere on God's prophetic radar. Gather those who will rise and carry the mantle of Christ forward and into this new era. This prophetic blueprint is a must-read for access into the power realm and understanding the interconnection of Prophets and Deliverance.

Courtney M. Beacham, Chief Prophet
Jesus People Proclaim International Church
Boca Raton, Florida

# FROM THE AUTHOR

I wrote Prophets and Deliverance as a model for prophetic people. I noticed differences between prophets, and their uniqueness captivated me. The execution and personification of some prophets are oracular, while others seem organizational or scribal. Nevertheless, I do not want to be prophetic based on cultural influence. This ascertainment is when my prophetic course took a detour.

We are different agents with specific auxiliaries created for a divine purpose. Maybe this is an eye-opener for those who have been trying to fit in. The question is, why try to fit? Perhaps, you do not because you cannot. That is my gift to you – to help you resolve that your difference is for purpose, destiny, and kingdom utilization.

There is a saying that goes, when the student is ready, the teacher shows up. I did not know it at the time, but an inquisition caused a dimensional shift in me. As a result, I encountered two things, heavenly bliss, and warfare. I learned lessons of faith, patience, and love. I also relearned vital foundational lessons.

At one point, and for many reasons, I became relaxed concerning my prophetic call. I neglected my basic-training and paid the price with sleepless nights, torment, physical exhaustion, demonic dreams, and horrific encounters. I lost ground (faith-wise). Yep! I said it. I, Judith John, started a downward fall towards doubt for reasons that most would not admit. Despite it all, I was set free from the law of sin and death through receiving the mind of Christ (Philippians 2:5).

A while back, I opened the doors to the demonic realm in two ways. The first was when I dated a freemason turned Christian. About three months into our courtship, I had a dream. I was unclear about the dream, but I knew it was a warning. I called a pastor-prophet to ask for guidance about what I dreamed. He said that I was too guarded, and God wanted me to lighten up. He said, "God wants you to know that your past is your past and what you experienced with your ex is gone." I believed in the man of God. So, I dismissed what I knew deep inside and moved on. Long story short, some unfortunate events occurred. His counsel was problematic because he said the infamous phrase, God said. The other problem was that I disregarded the one truth I knew; my dream was a warning. The pastor-prophet spoke words of exhortation and edification, but they were erroneous. His influence superseded my spiritual discernment. It was a mistake that I never wanted to relive.

A couple of Thanksgivings ago, the second door opened up. I was starting to recover from what I had endured the year before with the former freemason. So,

I was grateful for family, fellowship, and life. After we ate and ate some more, it was movie time. I asked my children what they wanted to watch. My youngest immediately responded, Harry Potter. Without hesitation, I agreed.

She and my youngest son snuggled in my bed to begin watching Harry Potter and the Sorcerer Stone. Soon after, both kids were fast asleep, and I was to finish Harry Potter alone. For some reason, the movie was captivating. I was intrigued by the storyline, the supernatural elements, and I obsessed over the symbolism. The next day I woke up, fixed a plate of leftovers, and watched Harry Potter the Chamber of Secrets. Ultimately, I watched all the listed Potter movies on our movie platform. Was I addicted to an occult-based series? Because this is not a memoir or autobiography, I would not go into more detail. However, the levels of demonic torment that I endured were just as bad as the year before. I learned hard lessons about idolatry, secularism, occultic material, soul impressions, delusion, and inner wounds. Mostly, I figured out that I was looking for something that people could not give me. I had a fascination for the supernatural, but I could not use the intelligence of dark arts.

One of the worst things we can do is to become enthralled with the ethereal through dark expression. If we do, our soul alters, and an opening occurs to allow access to our inner man. The information about portal traveling and how the character had ascertained new levels intrigued me. However, the source had the potential to corrupt me. Please understand that informational gain is not nefarious, but impure information opens us up or awakens our soul to deposits.

In the Garden of Eden, Eve opened her soul to infringement. Her actions changed her Godly identity. The souls of Adam and Eve came subjected to a deposit that reproduced after its kind. Let me qualify my statement. Ladies and gentlemen, we are the sum of our thoughts! Informational deposits influence thinking. What we see, hear, or experience produces our environment. The atmospheric conditions in an expanse reveal what influences the soul. It is how we produce our kind or likeness in the physical and metaphysical sense.

One Scripture says, "as a man thinks in his heart, so is he" (Proverbs 23:7). The term thinks means shaar (Strong's number 8176). It implies to split open, reason out, or reckon. And "in his heart" means nephesh (Strong's number 5313), indicating a soul, living being, life, self, person, desire, appetite, and emotion. Therefore, the words of the serpent reshaped Eve's soul. Although her outward appearance remained the same, she was conforming to another image. Words are seeds of influence, just like the Word of God. The

Harry Potter script influenced me, although I was unaware. It was as if my soul produced invisible keys that unlocked my life to demonic realms. In the end, Christ recovered me. After a year of devilish torment and a series of failed and productive deliverance sessions, the power of salvation saved me again.

I wrote "Prophets and Deliverance" for many reasons. On my recovery journey, I read books and met with ministers, pastors, apostles, and prophets who were not helpful. Some used witchcraft methods to administer deliverance. Others told me that I would be in spiritual warfare forever because I willfully opened the door. Clergy workers could not discern how to help me. At one point, I wanted death. The demons took over my dream realm. I heard their conversations about me at night and early in the morning. When they were not talking about me, they were talking to me. Shouting things like, you will die like this! We are never leaving! Didn't you pray to God? He is not coming! Other times, they assaulted me while I slept, both sexually and physically.

I fasted, prayed, drove to conferences, and paid money for deliverance sessions, only to walk away from an unsuccessful experience. I discovered that the Holy Spirit's gifts were not working in the deliverance workers I visited. Some of the people I met with who wrote books on deliverance had no discernment. Finally, after months of searching, God sent three people to help me overcome different deliverance stages. One was a woman of God out of Chicago, the second was an Apostle in Georgia, and the third was a prophet in the northern part of the U.S. I knew that the first gift all believers gained at the time of salvation was the Holy Ghost. So, I was baffled. I questioned the power of God among people.

These experiences resulted in a heart for a separated life. But, I had many questions. Long before my call to the office of a prophet, I noticed things others did not. I wanted to know how and why I could see or discern, especially during times of prayer. I yearned to understand how God built me as a prophet. Research, experience, prayer, and the Holy Spirit are my reasons for writing Prophets and Deliverance. Most importantly, my lessons cultivated a heart and allegiance to Yahweh-God.

This book is for the audience of believers who want clarity on the prophetic spheres and deliverance, but more importantly, a set-apart life unto Christ. I never dreamed of the encounters that I had experienced. Furthermore, the truth is that I knew something big was coming.

### Prophetic and Warning Dream

God gave me a dream during the two years that I

experienced hardship. Nevertheless, this time, I took the dream to God, and not a man. I knew that the dream was dual, a warning and a prophetic dream.

I dreamt that I took my car for routine maintenance. I got out of my car and went to the customer service desk. The lady at check-in was from Haiti. I said I'm here to drop off my car. She looked at me with disdain, blinked her eyes repeatedly, and dismissed me. Her customer service was horrible. But ignored her and left my keys at the front desk with the maintenance attendant. My youngest son went to the bathroom, and I went up the stairs.

On the way up, I passed another Haitian woman on the second floor. She was a witch. When our eyes met, she looked at me angrily. Again, I dismissed the lousy treatment and went to the third floor of the building. I saw baby clothes everywhere, and the store reminded me of a Sears Department Store. I went to the boy section and picked out baby clothes. Not long after, a Haitian man with a large belly walked up to me, also vexed. He glared at me, waiting for me to acknowledge him. I looked around the store, and no one was there except him and me. Somehow, I knew he was evil. Either he was a Voodoo priest or a witch doctor. Either way, he was a part of the occult, but I did not know which craft he mastered. I remembered thinking he wants to frighten me. So, I stood boldly and said, "I know who you are, but you do not scare me. I am not a fake Christian." He responded in Kreyol, "I am coming for you," and he walked away angrier. I packed the rest of the baby clothes and went back downstairs. Strangely, everyone was gone except my children. I called out to my son in the bathroom, let's go! When we got outside, I realized that my car turned into a black extra-long sport utility vehicle. My oldest attempted to jump into the driver's seat, but I told him that I would drive. When we pulled out, all the roads were white. I had no idea where we were. I proceeded to go, trusting that we would make it to our destination, and I woke up.

This dream was prophetic and a warning. I recognized that I was in a time of warfare and unavoidable confrontation connected to my Haitian heritage. I also understood that something new was on the way. Upgrades, as well as uncertainty, would meet me on the journey ahead. Nevertheless, most of all, my family would experience the new with me. On my way up, in the dream, I experienced terrible customer service from craft workers. At the top, a master of the craft confronted me, and I could not ignore it. He represented my past and present warfare as well as the warfare I would encounter. Nonetheless, the vehicle upgrade came to support the encounters and the path my family and I would take together. Though our way would not be familiar, faith would be essential on the road we would travel. I encourage you to find out where you are on your prophetic journey. This way, you can pray and ask God for guidance, grace, support, and Godly connections to journey well.

The prophetic is a realm of communication. Whether the communication is audio, visual, signs, or discernment, this is one of God's primary ways to speak to humanity. The prophetic is not something to fear. Instead, it is divine. We can learn about the prophetic by looking at the books of Daniel, Ezekiel, Revelations, and other books of the bible. Numbers 12:6 is one of the prophetic scriptures which substantiates prophetic initiation. 2 Kings 9:1-3 and 1 Samuel 10:11 explain the idea of a prophetic company and prophetic assignment.

The prophetic illuminates the hidden. But there are a few basics that indicate readiness.
- Christian discipleship
- Prophetic training
- Learning natural and spiritual protocol
- Master professionalism
- Overcoming bias ideas of love
- Displaying the fruit of the Spirit

And other vital character traits and developments. Godly prophetic communication is about how you communicate what you see, hear, or discern. To debate whether someone is a prophet or not is futile. How their prophetic is delivered is more valuable to the cause of Christ and Christianity. And the how determines the inner workings of a prophet and if they engage the prophetic spheres properly. Deliverance, on the other hand, is the handiwork of God. One of my favorite scriptures says, "But, if we drive out demons by the finger of God, then the kingdom of God has come near to you" (Luke 11:20).

Deliverance is not merely about human effort. It is the enactment of God's kingdom that manifests on earth. Some of the shenanigans that I endured while in some deliverance sessions were because people wrote books and preached in theory rather than exhibiting God's kingdom's power. The scripture that says, "Having a form of godliness but denying its power. Have nothing to do with such people," was real to me. In time past, I was a sincere zealot for deliverance ministry. However, now I understand that deliverance is more about redemption and salvation than expelling demons from people's lives. Here goes my disclaimer, I did not say that deliverance ministries are not necessary. However, our focus must be on God's kingdom, our source of power and dominion. Also, on Christ -Jesus, our Savior and kingdom connection. Other principles are discussed later in the chapters to follow.

## Chapter 1 The Soul

Souly Overturning Legislative Effects of Falsehoods, a.k.a. S.O.L.E., means facing the foundational issues in the soul of humanity. Some say that the human soul is the mind, the will, and the individual's emotions. However, why and what is the basis for these implications? Legislation in a country contributes to societal norms. And lawmakers have the power to influence their citizens. When legislators are corrupt, the systems governed by them are primarily affected. Consequently, many unfortunate things may happen in such a culture. Culture describes the customs, arts, social institutions, and achievements of a particular nation, people, or other social groups. Therefore, the soulish structure in such a government allows and disallows corporate behavior. The core beliefs at the center of a person's thinking affect his or her total being. Therefore, souly overturning the old legislative effects is paramount in recovering and redeeming humanity.

## Defining the Soul

The soul is man's personhood. I heard that the soul of a person is his or her truest part. If this is true, how do the *nephesh* (soul) and *psuche* (psyche) relate to one another biblically? Moreover, what is the difference between a human being and other created beings? Is it merely intelligence, or is there more to humanity outside of anatomy?

Darwin's Law of Evolution is a theory that proposes human existence is the byproduct of evolved organisms. However, the human soul is metaphysical. Furthermore, human appetite, passions, emotions, and other personhood supersedes organismal evolution. Matthew 10:28 says, "Do not be afraid of those who kill the body but cannot kill the soul. Instead, fear the one that can destroy both soul and body in hell."

The word soul is translated contextually as psuche. However, the soul has six other terms that define it: chay, ruwach, nephesh, zoe, pneuma, and psucho. In context, psuche represents the soul, life, and self (Strong's Exhaustive Concordance, #5590). More specifically, 5590 corresponds precisely to the OT H5315/phago (soul). The soul is the direct aftermath of God breathing his life into a person, making them an ensouled being (Helps Word Studies).

## The Making of Humanity

Genesis helps us understand the making of earthly creation. The creatures, beast, and other living things find their origin in the book of Genesis. Nevertheless, how did humanity come alive? A famous scripture says, "And the Lord God formed man of the dust of the ground and breathed into the nostrils the breath of life, and man became a living soul" (Gen. 2:7). Two extraordinary things occurred on the sixth day of creation. First, God formed Adam's physical anatomy and the systems within his human framework (respiratory, nervous, muscular, digestive, lymphatic, skeletal, and other systems). Not to mention vital organs and dependency on elements like oxygen, water, light, and food. God created the physique perfectly.

Next, God gave Adam *chay*, translated to English as life. The human body or container came to life and was living and breathing. God's breath caused Adam to become a living soul. Though *chay* describes life or age, humans have "a part" outside of their physical makeup called the inner man. In context, *chay* means life or vitality. However, other versions interpret *chay* as a living being, living soul, and living creature to explain life. Life and soul were not separate during creation. God blows more than air into Adam's body.

## The Physical Meets the Spiritual

The *psuche* of humankind is connected to the innerman and not necessarily the anatomy of man. The inward man is like a container inside of a container. 2 Corinthians 4:16 says, "Therefore we do not lose heart. Though outwardly we are wasting away, yet inwardly we are renewed day by day". Our outer container eventually dies and returns to dust. However, what we do in this life will determine where our inner man spends eternity.

The inner or inward man is the container that holds the *psuche*. Just like the body contains the brain, heart, and kidneys, the soul includes systems too. Jesus said, "Love the Lord, your God with all your heart, with all your soul, with all your mind, and with all your strength" (Mark 12:30). Translated: Love the Lord, your God with all your *kardias*, with all your *psuche*, all your *dianoias*, and with all your *ischus*.

*Kardia* translates as the heart. It is the effective center of our being and the capacity of moral preferences. P. Hughes says that "The heart is our volitional desire and choice." G. Archer presumes that the heart is a "desire producer that makes us tick." He called it our "desire-*decisions*" that establish who we are (HELPs Word-studies). The heart is mentioned over 800 times in Scripture but never referring to the literal physical pump that drives the blood. That is, "heart" is only used figuratively both in the O.T. and N.T. It is known as the seat of human life in both senses.

*Dianoia* translates as the imagination, the mind, and understanding (Strong's Exhaustive Concordance). *Dianoia* consists of the dia and the nous. It means deep thought, correctly through the faculty of the mind or its disposition, by implication. Its exercises imagination and understanding. Finally, *Ischus* is from *isxys* - formerly used as the term "force to overcome immediate resistance" (HELPS Word-studies). Kardias, psuche, dianoias, and ischus are the inner man's systems. Hence, the part that is terra-firma and the part that is nonphysical merge together as a binding human form.

## In the Beginning

Humanity's mental capacity is vast, and the mind exists to aid in the decision-making process. Therefore, a person's core value or beliefs is the foundational framework for healthy and prosperous existence. However, many things can influence the mind, including the flesh, outside sways, or the Holy Spirit. The bible says, "The carnal mind is death, but the mind governed by the Spirit is life and peace" (Romans 8:6). Contextually, the flesh or the outer container represents a person's sensual or human nature and relates to parental, cultural, or environmental influences.

We find many impactful events throughout the Bible, and the book of Genesis happens to reveal one significant effect that changed the course of humanity forever. In the beginning, God created many creations, including Adam. God made many trees in the garden where Adam would live. However, the tree of the knowledge of good and evil was forbidden (Genesis 2:17). Specifically, God told Adam that he would die if he eats from the tree of good and evil knowledge. Consider that Adam had the ability to *dianoia (to have deep thought, to exercise* decision). In Eden, Adam had one influence that he obeyed until another influence arrived (Genesis 3:6). God created one more person and gifted her as a helpmate. Though Adam and Eve were different persons, their allegiance was with God. Their commitment originated in oneness with Him. However, the serpent introduced a new idea with wicked intentions. As he talked with Eve, he asked, "Did God say that you should not eat of any tree in the garden?" She replied, we can eat, just not from the tree amid the garden; don't even touch it, or we'll die. You won't die, said the serpent. "For God knows that in the day you eat of it, your eyes will be opened, and you will be like God, knowing good and evil" (Genesis 3:6). What was the serpent's plan? What did he know that Adam and Eve did not?

### Authentic Dominion

Be reminded of how God released *chay* (life) into the man's clay body. Adam became a container filled with life. Next, God named his creation. Naming Adam caused a couple of things to happen. One, He gave

Adam identity. Two, He proved ownership. Furthermore, Adam received authentic dominion on earth. To seal Adam's rule, God brought the living creatures to Adam. He named them and confirmed his authority over them (Gen. 2:19).

When the serpent talked with Eve, he had a plan. He chose words that would change the idea of her identity forever. The physical and metaphysical parts of Adam and Eve were perfect. Nevertheless, the serpent suggested that God limited them, making them insufficient. Satan used the old trick of deception, influencing Eve's mind by withholding the truth and coercing her to choose based on a falsehood. Satan knew that Adam's dominion connected to how God formed his body and his inner man. His earth-formed container with the God-breathed life made him an ensouled person, which had the force and power to overcome immediate resistance through reasoning. Being made in God's likeness and image authorized Adam as an official representative of God on earth. Some argue that women are subservient to men because of Eve's susceptibility to the serpent. However, before Eve's encounter with the snake, God brought Eve to Adam. He named her like he did the creatures in the garden. I digress.

If humans lost their molecular structure, they would be a different being, but a "being" nonetheless.

Astral projection is how a person leaves their molecular structure. More commonly, it is known as an out-of-body experience. It is an art that involves intense meditation, and humans learn to abandon the body and travel the ethereal. The mind does not remain with the body when astral projecting. The mind is the reason the spirit and soul can dislodge from the outer container.

Notice that the body is dead without the mind, but the mind drives the spirit and soul. The spirit (pneuma) cannot go without the soul (nephesh). Hence, power is not necessarily in either container but resonates with our ability to think. "For as a man thinks in his heart (nephesh), so is he" (Proverbs 23:7). Ladies and gentlemen, you are your nephesh!

The condition of the soul predicates on a person's state of mind. The mind influences the inner and outer container, which determines the human experience. Matthew 10:28 says, "Do not fear those who kill the body but cannot kill the soul. But rather, fear Him, who can destroy both soul and body in hell."

In context, the term *psuche* describes the soul instead of *nephesh*. But what makes *psuche* and *nephesh* similar? Look at the chart and compare psuche and nephesh. Afterward, see how they correspond or differ from one another. (see chart)

| 5590. Psuche – soul, life, self | 5315. Nephesh – a soul, living being, life, self, person, desire, passion, appetite, emotion |
|---|---|
| Breath, the soul<br>Usage: (a) vital breath, a breath of life, (b) the human soul, (c) the soul as the seat of affections and will, (d) the self, € a human | 1. that which breaths, the breathing substance or being = soul, anima, the soul, the inner being of man:<br>2. the living being by God's breathing.<br>3. the soul (without an animal noun or |

| | |
|---|---|
| person, an individual (Strong's Concordance) | verb) is specified: a. a living being whose life resides in the blood. b. a severe attack upon the life is an attack upon the inner living being. 4 The soul as the essence of man stands for the man himself. a. Paraphrase for personal pronoun, especially in poetry and ornate discourse. b. Reflective self c. person of man, individual Five soul = seat of appetites, in all periods. a. Hunger: hungry soul b. Thirst: weary soul c. appetite in general 6. Seat of emotions and passions a. Desire: soul desire b. Abhorrence, loathing c. Sorrow and distress: bitter, gloomy, discontented of soul d. joy of my soul rejoices e. Love f. Alienation, hatred, revenge g. Other emotions and feelings (Brown-Driver-Briggs) |
| From *psyxo*, "to breathe, blow," which is the root of the English words "phyche," "psychology" – soul (psyche); a person's distinct identity (unique personhood), i.e., individual personality. Corresponds to the OT 5315. Phago (soul). The soul is the direct aftermath of God breathing His gift of life into a person, making them an ensouled being (HELPS Word-studies) | Any, thyself, them your-selves, slay, soul, tablet, they, thing, from *naphash* (to be refreshed) (Strong's Concordance) |
| Soul, life, self From *psucho* (to breathe, blow, to make cool); breath, i.e. (by implication) spirit, abstractly or concretely (the animal sentient principle only; thus, distinguished on the one hand from pneuma (wind, breath, | Be refreshed. A primitive root to breathe passively, to breathed upon, i.e. (figuratively) refreshed (as if by a current of air) – (be) refresh selves (-ed) (Strong's Exhaustive Concordance) |

spirit), which is the rational or immortal soul; and on the other from *Zoe* (life, both physical (present) and of spiritual (particularly future) existence), which is merely vitality, even of plants: these terms thus exactly correspond respectively to the Hebrew *nephesh, ruwach,* and *chay*)
(Strong's Exhaustive Concordance)

These two words are progressives. The term *nephesh* stands on *naphesh*. On the other hand, the *psuche* expresses the progression of the latter. Humankind's *psuche* sustains life for the body and soul. It also functions as the psyche. It is the thinking mechanisms that make individuals different although accountable for personal actions. The mind, will, and emotions sum up the soul. However, the soul is our being and vice versa. Therefore, what we do with our mind, our will, and our emotions determine the path we travel. Adam and Eve are an example of directional change based on the trajectory of their souls. However, God has a recovery plan to mend the soul and course of humanity.

### Souly Overthrow the Legislation in Effect

Adam and Eve's earthly connections were legal and irrevocable. However, the adversary planned and calculated how he would *souly* overthrow the legislation in effect (S.O.L.E.) on the earth. Since he could not destroy the legislature in heaven, the earth was the next best place. The rightful representatives on the planet were Adam and Eve, but Satan calculated how he could influence them and legally take possession of the earth. In heaven, Satan's attempted takeover was unsuccessful, so he needed a different approach. It is not easy to subvert legalities, but if Satan could get the earth representatives to vote informally, he would be the new owner. Though voting today is usually done by submitting a ballot, it is also a choice between two or more candidates or courses of action. Deciding on something or choosing to do something is counted as a vote. The expression which says not choosing is still a choice is also valid. Whether Adam and Eve knew it or not, Satan was in the running for their choice. He might not have been the popular choice, but they voted for his idea when they acted in disobedience.

Satan's suggestions led to the authorized transaction of legal rights. Eve left her position intellectually though her physical location never changed. Was this not the same principle Satan used to win the angels turned agents of darkness? They held their physical position in heaven while still pretending to serve Yahweh. Nevertheless, they were like the people in Isa. 29:13 and Matthew 15:8. In both scriptures, the heart is translated as kardias, meaning thoughts and feelings. Their views were turned from God, denoting that their singleness or identicalness was compromised.

The serpent was after the oneness or synchronization of Adam's thoughts towards God. Before Satan's influence, Adam and Eve were in one thought with God. Nevertheless, sin separated them and disconnected Adam from his creational right of dominance as the sitting authority on earth.

## Where It All Began

Revelations 12 explains the warfare Lucifer (the Dragon) began in heaven. Michael and his angels fought against the rebellious Dragon. He and his angels were defeated. The bible says, "He was thrown down, that ancient serpent, called the devil and Satan, the deceiver of the whole world – he was thrown down to earth, and his angels were thrown down with him." Satan influenced a third of the angels in heaven. That was just shy of one half of the heavenly host.

One of the easiest ways to influence a person is through the mind. What causes a person to think? What he hears and what he sees stimulates thinking, generating a response in the face of decisions. Therefore, intellectualism does not necessarily mean correct or smart. In context, it means to calculate in the soul and chose. Thus, intellectualism is conceptualization. The elements around us shape our emotions, intellect, thoughts, and behaviors. The most influential time of shaping is in the womb, infancy, and childhood, but this is not the only time. Peer pressure, observation, and stimulation also influence the mind. The mind remembers the good, the bad, the ugly in the temporal lobe, the happy birthday parties, the lonely holidays, and all in-between. Though memories help humans create behaviors, they also empower emotions. Babies learn how to adapt to their surroundings through trial and error. Learned behavior is forged over time to reinforce these memories. Children remember things that adults forget quickly. Like when an infant nestles up to mom, she separates emotionally or physically by placing an item between the infant and herself. The baby learns separation or independence. Furthermore, if a toddler reaches up for dad, he is picked up and greeted with a smile, then the child learns healthy affection and acceptance. These things are learned, experienced, and stored as memories to eventually produce behavior.

Satan's influence presented a crossroad for Adam and Eve. None of us know how long Eve talked with the serpent. Nor do we know how Lucifer convinced his angels. What we do know is that their thinking changed. The disobedient angels are described as *his* angels because their course of action validated their vote. Lucifer persuaded the fallen angels and Adam and Eve to disobey, which led to rebellion. "Let each be fully convinced in his mind" (Romans 14:5).

Believe it or not, disobedience is to rebel or to stand against what is in existence. In this case, there are two things to consider, systems (government) and authority (power; delegation). Behold, I give you the *exousia* to tread on serpents and scorpions. Overall, the *dunamis* (strength, power, might) of the enemy and nothing shall by any means hurt you (Luke 10:19). The mind is everything in warfare. Therefore, watch and protect your mind from unlawful influences (Matthew 16:19; 2 Peter 2:8). You can become the righteous influence of the Lord.

## Faith and the Mind

"You were taught, regarding your former way of life, to put off your old self, which is being corrupted by its deceitful desires, to be made new in the spirit of your minds" (Ephesians 4:23 -24). Be renewed in the spirit (*pneuma*) of your mind (*nous*). *Nous* is our Godly capacity to think (reason). It is also our mental dimensions, and we exercise reflective thinking by way of the *nous*. "For the believer, *nous* is the organ of receiving Godly thoughts through faith" (Helps Wordstudies, G3563. Nous). For Christians, the Holy Spirit influences our *nous* if we surrender our will. Once again, our willingness to yield or not brings us to a vote. Faith is unseen, but it has power through our thought to bring substance to evidence. In other words, faith becomes a physical matter. To manifest the Hebrews 11:1 proclamation, we cannot let uncertainty influence us.

Our conduct proves our alignment or misalignment with God and his kingdom. The serpent engaged Eve's mind, will, and emotions before the fall, which is the same fight Christians face today. Understanding the soul's complexity can help Christians administer deliverance and soul healing to those under Satan's influence.

Some of the earliest forms of idolatry go back to the days of Israel. Foreign gods, golden calves, and graven images are the baseline for God's wrath. Abraham's father worshiped other gods. Some speculate that the sun was amongst the images he favored (Joshua 24:2). King Solomon is an example of a governmental influence that allowed idolatry to turn a nation from Elohim.

## Chapter 2 Sinful Doorways

### Fundamentals of Idolatry

One reference of idolatry is tied back to the sins of King Solomon. The Bible expresses that Solomon had wives and concubines. The number was at least one-thousand women, including 700 wives and 300 concubines. 1 Kings 11:4 –9 was the premise used to substantiate judgments against Israel. "When Solomon was old, it came to pass that his wives turned away his heart after other gods. His heart was not perfect with the Lord his God, as was the heart of David, his father. Solomon went after Ashtoreth, the goddess of Zidonians (Sidonians), after Milcom (Molek), the Ammonites abomination. And likewise, did he for all his strange wives, which burnt incense and sacrificed unto their gods. Moreover, the Lord was angry with Solomon because his wives turned his heart from the Lord God of Israel, which appeared to him twice."

1 Kings 11:4-9 confirms judgments against Israel. It described idolatry, people-pleasing, and lust. Moreover, because of Solomon's sins, God pronounced that Israel would be torn away from King Solomon. The Lord also raised adversaries against him; one named Hadad and the other Rezon the son of Eliada (v.14 & v.23). Finally, someone outside of David's lineage would become king over ten tribes of Israel.

## Doorways to Other Influences

This story describes different forms of lust. However, people-pleasing and sexual immorality are two idolatries from Solomon's story that we will discuss. People-pleasing is a habit that lures one obsessing over another into idolatry. It can be an intense yearning that causes feelings of ambition, acceptance, and fulfillment, more commonly known as desire. People-pleasing is also an act of having many lords. Today the boss is their Lord, and tomorrow the pastor is Lord. If the people-pleasing habit is uncontrolled, his or her gaze will continue to lust after acceptance rather than surrendering to the adoption of Christ.

Lust, on the other hand, is the term epithymeo in Greek (G1937). Made up of two different words, G1909- on or upon, and G2372- passion. G1909 transposes to Epi. It is a preposition meaning many things, including "a focus on" and "intensifying." Furthermore, G2372 is translated to thumos, meaning an outburst of passion and wrath. J. Thayer says passion means rushed along, getting heated up, and breathing violently. Additionally, passion drives behavior. For instance, "actions emerging out of strong impulses or intense emotion" (HELPS Word-studies). Another word for desire is fierceness, indignation, and wrath (The Strong's Exhaustive Concordance). Therefore, lust describes other things besides sexual acts. Murders happen in the *outburst of passion*. Abuse can also occur when people get *heated up*. Their strong impulses cause lust to manifest in horrible ways, sometimes leading to death. Ephesians 4:26-27 (T.P.T.) says, "Do not let the passion of your emotions lead you to sin! Do not let your anger control you or be fuel for revenge, not even for a day. Do not allow the slanderous devil to manipulate you."

Lust is a driver. Usually, a wound and painful memories are present, whether this is realized or not. So, the person's life looks a little bit like a minivan. Lust drives, pain rides shotgun, wounds hang out in the first row while the inner and outer container goes along for the ride. Along the way, lust makes stops for gratification. These actions produce fanatic tendencies and are where the worship of objects comes into play.

Idolatry is the worship of an object or something visible. In Solomon's case, physical statues were erected and worshiped in place of our living God. Paul describes idolatry in Romans 1:21-25. "For although they knew God, they refused to give Him glory and thanksgiving. Therefore, the thoughts and hearts of

God's people shifted towards the idols." So, the same consequences Adam and Eve suffered were about to repeat. Eve and Solomon's strong desires changed the chain of command.

## Change in Leadership

Solomon's lusts caused a change in leadership. 1 Kings 11:26 introduced Jeroboam, a man who worked hard and well for Solomon. He was named to inherit an entire nation of people. Elohim used Prophet Ahijah to announce the change in government. One day Ahijah met Jeroboam while traveling. The prophet ripped his new garment into twelve pieces. He gave ten to Jeroboam and said, "Thus says the Lord, the God of Israel, 'Behold, I am about to tear the kingdom from the hand of Solomon (v.34). Nevertheless, I will not take the whole kingdom out of his hand, but I will make him ruler all the days of his life, for the sake of David, my servant whom I chose, who kept my commandments and my statutes." (vv.37-39).

"And I will take you, and you shall reign over all your soul (nephesh) desires. You shall be king over Israel. Furthermore, if you listen to all I command you and will walk in my ways, and do what is right in my eyes, by keeping my statutes and commandments, as David my servant did, I will be with you, and build you a sure house, as I built for David, and I will give Israel to you. Furthermore, I will afflict the offspring of David because of this, but not forever." (1 King 11:34-39).

Change in leadership is inevitable when humanity clings to idols.

Another sin is an unrepentant heart, known as stiffness or stubbornness. When Prophet Ahijah told Solomon what the Lord said, he hardened his heart and tried to murder Jeroboam. However, Jeroboam escaped and stayed in Egypt until Solomon died. Prophecy did not help Solomon see his errors. Instead, he tried to stop the inevitable with attempted murder. A stiff heart triggers projection. He displaced emotions as a defense mechanism to avoid his issues. In turn, he lost his inheritance and his father's blessings.

Finally, Solomon never tore down the idols in the high places. Sadly, he chose to worship created things rather than worship God the Creator (Romans 1:25). The Bible warns us about having a stubborn heart. It says, "Harden not thy heart as in the provocation, and as in the day of temptation in the wilderness. It is a people who err in their heart, and they have not known my ways" (Psalm 95:8-11). Solomon was stubborn, and his lust kept him delusional about who he became. Repentance and a yielded heart are premises that exclude stubbornness.

## Leadership & Identity

Praying for God's Kingdom and will on planet earth is a massive key concerning our existence. Whether humans decide to yield to this idea is an individual decision. "Thy kingdom come. Thy will be done in earth, as it is in heaven," is a famous scripture (Matthew 6:10). Solomon missed the idea of God's will or, in his case, God's commandment. Part of humanity's existence links to *chay*. However, when we misuse chay, we display the influence of vain ideas, toxic emotional behaviors, and lustful desire. Therefore, we disconnect from God's *chay* and our God-approved identity and dominion (*Kratos*) on earth. An essential part of humanity's existence is a connection to our Creator (Isaiah 40:28). Creation reflects its Creator when fueled by Godly intent and purpose. *Kratos* works best for those who yield to the plan of God's purposefulness. If a person's goal is misguided, *Kratos* works against the purposes and promises of God.

Unfortunately, what happened in Solomon's time is also happening today. More shockingly, it is happening in the house of the Lord. People who worship tribalism, music, culture, money, athletes, patriotism, the past (nostalgia), family (nepotism), fraternal/sorority gods, and of course, self-worship use their *Kratos* recklessly. God's house can represent three things: the physical man, the inner man, and the church - as in the *body* of believers, and a building.

Kratos – force, strength, power, might: mighty with great power. Dominion (Strong's number G2904)

## Idolatry and the Church

Idol worship has led the church back into judgment for multiple reasons. Some of those are (1) Ignorance of the Scriptures, (2) Bigotry, (3) Disobedience, (4) Idolatry, and (5) Profanity & Mixture. There is a considerable debate about how we worship the Sovereign God. Some Christians practice and accept "cultural" beliefs about God's requirement for true worship. Rather than excepting what God deems as acceptable. We find his conditions in many scriptures throughout the Bible. "God is spirit, and they that worship Him must worship Him in spirit and truth" (John 4:24). Jesus also said, "You worship what you do not know... However, the hour is coming when the true worshipers will worship the Father in spirit and truth. For the Father is seeking such to worship Him" (vv.23-24). No other worship is acceptable.

Secularism has crept into the people and the houses of fellowship. Humans have become distant from God. So they desire Prophets or Psychics to tell them what the future holds. Will they be rich, or married, or have a great job and kids? Itching ears are what 2 Timothy 4:3 says. "The time will come when they will not endure sound doctrine but having itching ears. They shall heap to themselves teachers following their lust." Idolatry is the foundation of lustful desires. People choose to worship their worldly passions because that is what they feel or sense more than God.

The third sinful door is profanity or mixture. The term mixture defines the combination of more than one substance. True worship is not combined with anything, but it is pure, holy, and untouched by secularism. Secularism means practices that do not represent God's standards and laws. Secularism involves strong influences of culture and societal norms. We are a royal priesthood and living epistles for Christ's cause. So, our mandate is purity, holiness, and sanctification through the Holy Ghost. We are supposed to be the persuaded nation of God that diligently seeks Godly connection. But are we?

When priests overlook the unholy activities in the prayer houses of God, on the platforms, and behind the scenes, sin becomes fertile ground for corruption and contempt. The sanctity of God's holiness devalued by humanity causes tolerance. In many cultures, the specific locations to worship a deity happens in sanctuaries or temples. These temples are decorated and adorned based on the preferences of their beloved god. Any non-customary offering given in these sanctuaries is called heretical or blasphemous. The persons responsible are scorned, beaten, or forbidden to reenter the temple based on the culture's edict. The priests in the temples around the world do not permit mixture in the temples they shepherd. The same should be true of our bodily temple. The bible says, "What? Know ye not that your body is the temple of the Holy Ghost, which is in you, which you have of God, and you are not your own" (1 Corinthians 6:19).

## Satan's Agenda

Satan plans to corrupt God's holy mandate (ex. persons, places, and things) as he did before the flood in Genesis. If he succeeds and corrupts the embryo (foundation) of a system, he can penetrate the people's coding, D.N.A., and land. In the Garden of Eden, Satan influenced the plans of God through humans. He re-coded/reset the pattern of dominion. The course of humanity needed a complete reset after Satan's infiltration, and Jesus is the solution for society.

This point brings us to another door. Satan wants to possess or corrupt the land (territory, space, domain, etc.). After the infiltration in the Garden of Eden, another invasion occurred. The sons of God slept with the daughters of men. In other words, watchers/angels/otherworldly beings had sexual relations with human beings. These women gave birth to hybrid babies who had blended D.N.A. They were called the mighty men of old. When God saw Satan's plan's manifest, He caused a flood to wipe out the beings that were born through the mixture (Genesis 6:1-4). God thought about destroying everything he created, including humans, because of their sin and mixture. However, thank God for Noah (Genesis 6:8).

So, what do unholy priests produce today? It may not be Nephilim, but it will be something impure. The manifestation of impure seeds/coding is secularism. The existence of divergent individuals spreads throughout the population and eventually contaminates the watchmen, guardians, intercessors, and gatekeepers. Therefore, corruption eats at the land. Guardians are struck by friendly fire, and the people build idols under the defiled priest's eye. Exodus 32 describes Aaron as the leader who built the golden calf for God's people. The Bible says that Aaron made the people naked before their enemies (v.25). It was not a physical nakedness. No, the people were naked with "shameful sin." Israel kept going back to what they knew. They knew foreign gods, but they had not yet come to know the true and living God. The Bible says, "They know their God who shall be strong and do great exploits" (Daniel 11:32). So, their strength failed and their appetite for an idol prevailed. They desired a symbol of a god.

### Here's Your Symbol

People use mental pictures or ideas and statues, animals, angels, and other things as symbols of worship. The principality Jezebel waits to manipulate such people, especially those who might be susceptible to idol worship. Let us pause here. Jezebel was a queen in her time. Based on her lineage, characteristics, and persona, we find a spiritual influence repeatedly duplicated throughout history. Hence, creating a stronghold. Strongholds represent the intertwining connection developed by ruling principalities. So, the prosperity of a stronghold's rule secures a principality's dominance, also known as a prince

(Ephesians 2:2; Daniel 10:13). The term principality symbolizes spiritual unification in a territory—any ideas accepted in a society influence the environment. Therefore, a systematic policy forges and governs the people – hence, cultural impact. Thus, a system that resembles control, manipulation, accusation, murder, strong delusion, and weak leadership references a Jezebelic system.

Continuing, we see the vulnerability of ignorance. A Jezebelic system usually gathers individuals who suffer from two significant ailments - rejection and fear. Rejection and fear are normalities that we contend with every day we live life. Gone unchallenged, a person sees life through the lens of pain, self-defense, or hyper states (hyperalert, hypervigilant, etc.). Low self-esteem is another open door. As evil spirits visit people, eventually, they become victims of other more viable spirits. The following page provides a list of spiritual entities that can oppress, depress, or influence believers. This list is essential, as it will give intel on how spirits build strongholds.

# Disembodied Spirits or Personalities

| | | | |
|---|---|---|---|
| Negativity | Depression | Doubt | Haughtiness |
| Hate | Profanity | Fantasy | Abandonment |
| Promiscuity | Accusation | Heaviness | Lewdness |
| Orphan | Mockery | Contentious | Sabotage |
| Abusive | Lust | Sarcasm | Doubleminded |
| Sickness | Seduction | Torment | Pride |
| Vanity | Delusion | Hardhearted | Heavy Sorrow |
| Gossip | Manipulation | Affectation | Death |
| Lying | Bitterness | Anxiety | Envy |
| Recklessness | Busybody | Murder | Vagabond |
| Narcissism | Control | Unthankful | Perfection |
| Revelry | Prostitution | Divination | Selfishness |
| Licentiousness | Poverty | Unyielding | Fear |
| Rebellion | Rejection | Disobedience | Addiction |
| Prejudice | Laziness | Vain Imagination | Thief |
| Rage | Incest | Lethargy | Boasting |
| Witchcraft | Cursing | Cunningness | Jealousy |
| Possessiveness | Shame | Aimlessness | Passivity |
| Escapism | Defiance | False Burdens | Brainwashing |

This list can help while administering deliverance techniques. An example could be during deliverance, some will say, "I curse rejection. Leave now in Jesus' name, and nothing happens." However, the Holy Spirit says, "Tell manipulation to release its hold and boom! Manipulation leaves and fear is left exposed with no defense. Of course, the deliverance worker has no idea that the stronghold is fear, and the strong man is manipulation" (Mark 3:27). Now, the deliverance worker can minister to the person based on the revelation of the Holy Spirit.

Furthermore, the laws that give fear legal access/rights to the person's mind and life evacuate by the authority of Christ. When we minister to people, we help rewrite the thoughts that held the previous stronghold in place. Therefore, renewing the mind is our biggest weapon against our adversary. The deliverance worker or prophet's soul needs to be whole as well, or infiltration from the otherworldly will commence.

## Chapter 3 DELIVERANCE

### Part 1

Prophets and deliverance are like coffee and cream. Black coffee is good. However, coffee is better with a little cream added. This example is one way to explain how I see deliverance. Deliverance is functional in and of itself. However, the administration of deliverance work paired with prophetic insight brings about phenomenal results in both the natural and spiritual realms. Some people, including prophets, usually peer into the spiritual realms finding the prophetic sphere. However, the knowledge of the prophetic arena is not a qualification for employment or involvement.

Prophets are officers of more than the prophetic spheres. Their main job is to officiate in their expertise, accessing necessary understandings to accomplish their work through Godly authorization. These officers learn to administer deliverance variously, but they should learn through the Holy Spirit's teachings and scriptures. Though this is not always the case, the spirit of prophecy is one of God's deliverance tools.

The spirit of prophecy's entire responsibility is to testify of Jesus. As a missionary from heaven, Jesus had one goal, and he fulfilled it. His objective was to come and do the will of Abba (John 6:38). When the fall of Adam and Eve happened, our Father had a deep desire to rescue humanity from the deadly covenant forged through sin. Sin is as simple as a covenant with death (Genesis 2:17). I also need to mention that sin is disobedience in heaven or on earth. Both places are worlds with systems, government, and enforcement officers. When laws or rules are given to an individual, family, or a group of people, to act against those laws constitutes repercussion. So, whether one understands why instructions are in place holds no constraint on what produces afterward.

Adam and Eve had no real revelation of what God was saying when he spoke, "But you must not eat from the tree of knowledge of good and evil; for, in the day that you eat of it, you will surely die." Surely die? What is death to two people who never saw life end? Furthermore, they only understood evil knowledge after they ate from the tree. Adam experienced God's created life in Eden and nothing else. So, what is it to die? Adam and Eve soon discovered that sin creates separation and eventually death.

Obedience is the arch nemeses of sin and death. It is the one thing that will always trump the powers of darkness because of faith. Satan is the leader of the kingdom of darkness (Ephesians 2:2), and he preys on what we do not understand. I heard the late Dr. Miles Monroe say, "Ignorance is the absence of light." His revelation about light and darkness gave me clarity and a new perspective about sin and death. If at one time, we were dead because of sin, then death met us because we lacked insight and revelation, the representation of light. The Bible says, "At one time you were dead because of your sins (v.1). You followed the sinful ways of the world and obeyed the leader of darkness. He is the devil who is now working with the people who do not obey God (v.2). By his loving favor, you have been saved from the punishment of sin through faith (v.8)." Adam and Eve may not have had a revelation, but God was looking for faith.

Not little faith, but for Pistis faith, which means faithfulness (Strong's Concordance 4102). They both knew what God said, yet somehow, that ole' serpent was able to deceive the closest humans to God. A vital foundational lesson that you can carry with you throughout your prophetic journey is obedience is better than anything. Your compliance to God's scriptural word and Rhema will produce a byproduct of faithfulness. Submission to his words will prove that you can be faithful or Pistis when things are not obvious or sound. If God says anything, find out his timeframe, ask Him to provide the grace and wisdom to accomplish the task. Most importantly, please obey the Lord.

In the Bible, you will read accounts where people disobeyed God for a plethora of reasons. However, one issue that kills prophets is not knowing or understanding a thing—in other words, not having faith and wisdom. Sometimes, when prophets realize that they have a gift to see, discern, and articulate what God says, he or she can become comfortable or familiar with the normalcy of the prophetic and even God's company. Adam and Eve are an example of this. They became accustomed to Divine visitations, and their comfortableness led to their unfortunate eviction from the Garden of Eden. This scenario is as old as time, yet the prophets of God fall into similar traps. For what reasons would Adam and Eve have to be on guard? God visited them, spoke to them, and loved them immensely. In their world, there was no impending danger, so they thought.

Is this not the same with the prophets today? I hear things like, "God speaks to me all the time" or "God said x, y, z." However, when God speaks to them concerning their life, Pistis is not showing up—on the other hand, lacking a foundation of scriptural knowledge and wisdom can also prohibit effectiveness. Selah.

A part of Jesus' missionary mandate is to offer believers access to God's kingdom through salvation and revelation. Revelation is light that works with understanding and the wisdom of the Lord. What are the benefits of seeing a vision but lacking the ability to accomplish the vision? Habakkuk said, "I will stand on my watch, and set me upon the tower, and will watch to see what he will say to me, and what I will answer when I am reproved." Habakkuk would watch, perceive, consider what the Lord said. Then he would wait for the Lord to correct what he perceived. In this context, reproved is H8433, defined as a rebuke, correction, or reproof; also, it means impeach an argument. Habakkuk 2:1 reflects the official prophetic duty of Habakkuk. He positioned himself to see, hear, and be corrected. Therefore, he understood that his perception could be incorrect or biased. In Habakkah 2:2, the Lord answers Habakkah and makes things plain. Then verse 3 says, "For the vision is for an appointed time, but at the end, it will speak and not lie: though it tarries, wait for it; because it will surely come, it will not tarry." Vision is good. However, without the right timing and revelation, it could cause confusion.

The kingdom of God is where Jesus reigns, and even this revelation powers faith (Revelation 1:9). Do not think of revelation as something unknowable, but relatively as something that needs uncovering.

God's truth is divinely legitimate. It is the exactness of light and the **image** Jesus Christ revealed to man. Jesus said, "I am the way, and the truth and the life. No one comes to the Father except through me" (John 14:6). Always bear in mind God's truth aligns with Jesus the Christ.

### Light and Lesser Light

Are there lesser lights that humankind accepts as truth? Of course! Nevertheless, what separates God's truth from other premises is the source. Some religions focus on the Bible's topics rather than its full writing. However, this approach denies judicious loyalty. There are over 3,000 religious practices across the globe, not to mention millions of deities. Still, one act of sin sealed a covenant with death that Jesus the Christ ultimately overturned.

After Adam and Eve sinned, they knew nakedness as an improper state of being. "Being like God," according to the serpent's deceit, was not working out too well. Actions sealed their covenant with Satan. Adam and Eve had no clue that eating the fruit from the tree of good and evil knowledge aligned them with Satan. Their act of sin stole their innocence, identity, and home. Sin created new terms for their covenant agreement with God. Eve believed that she would see or know or have the ultimate revelation like God, but that was not the case. Now, God uses faith and revelation to draw us back to himself.

Revelation is used all over the globe for good and evil purposes alike. Still, God's plan prevails and lives on because Jesus accomplished his missionary assignment to grant the inhabitants of earth salvation, deliverance, and kingdom access. Revelation should connect to God (Ephesians 1:9). One rule of thumb is to check and affirm revelation through Holy Scripture.

Scripture brings knowledge, builds faith, and empowers the one who believes in the word (1 John 1:1-4).

## Promissory Note of Freedom

Jesus came to set the captive free (Luke 4:18). Freedom referenced in Luke 4:18 includes sight for the blind, pardons for captive prisoners, and liberty for oppressed or broken souls. The aforementioned is significant because Jesus broke physical and mental contracts enforced in the natural and spirit world.

When we agree on a thought, idea, plan, or other proposals, we seal it with action. Adam and Eve acted on Satan's thoughts, thereby consenting to unfavorable laws (Gen 3:1). "Did God say you must not eat from any tree in the garden?" A question that looms over the earth until today. Though chains and forced labor represent enslavement, mental slavery is also real. Negative thinking patterns, or as Dr. Natalie Olsen puts it, N.A.T.S. (negative automatic thoughts), are ways Satan enforces his contracts. Slavery can also represent infirmity. Sicknesses and disease affect the life span, human proficiency, and the enjoyment that one can or cannot experience. The scriptures also reference the inability to see. Blindness in Luke 4:18 signifies physical or mental blindness (Strong's Concordance 5185 tuphlos).

Nevertheless, Jesus came to pardon the enforcement of physical/mental oppression through salvation and deliverance (Luke 4:18), conquering everything that opposed the earth's inhabitants. And although enslavement ballets with humanity, the Lord provides an escape route through Christ.

## Tools: The Spirit of Prophecy and Atmospheres

In 1 Samuel 10:6, the Spirit of God rushed to Saul, and he prophesied. It is not unusual for the spirit of prophecy to emerge in a prophetic atmosphere or gathering. A prophetic atmosphere develops when mantles are in unison. This was the case of the company of prophets in 1 Samuel 10. Saul encountered a set atmosphere. He was affirmed and confirmed by the Spirit of God, followed by prophetic acts.

Atmospheres are created by what is spoken or done in an environment: like prayer, praise, worship, declarations, and oaths. Notice all these acts use air or breath to establish what the environment will hold. So, the air in a territory begins to contain what is distributed by people. When we worship, we change the current atmosphere by renaming what we want in a space. When Saul met the prophets, they already pierced the spheres and created an atmosphere (in the air) conducive to activate portals. Let me challenge you with a question. Could it be that they were the portals? Before verse six, the prophet Samuel prophesied to

Saul that he would meet a company of prophets going to Bethel, receive two loaves of bread as a gift and that he would prophesy. Verse six further declares that Saul turned into a new man.

The Spirit of God is another key to successful deliverance. Men and women who rely on Christ and the Holy Spirit are successful because human experience is not their measuring stick.

Deliverance is not new. Expelling entities from places or dwellings is older than the written word of God. Multiple scripture references throughout the O.T. and N.T. substantiates deliverance. One well-known instance of satoria was the Israelites' exodus from the Egyptian rulers and their harsh punishment. After ten plagues and many conversations with Pharaoh, God delivered the Israelites from the toiling labors impressed by the Egyptian citizens. Exodus 12:13 says, "God smote the land of Egypt." When God said, I will smite the land." He meant that he would destroy or severely injure the territory, its legal decrees, and its sovereign's official power.

An important lesson about land is that it is purchased and owned. Believe it or not, believers are purchased as well, which denotes ownership. Galatians 3:13-14 says, "Christ brought us with His blood and made us free from the law. Moreover, for that reason, the law could not punish us." It is also written, "Anyone who hangs on a cross is hated and punished." Because of Christ, the good things that came to Abraham can come to people who are not Hebrew or Jewish.

Dozens of prophetic deliverance workers whom I spoke with agreed on one thing. Once they received deliverance, they wanted others to be free as well. I was acquainted with deliverance-work because, at one time, I was a deliverance worker. In times past, I administered deliverance from the stance of what I saw others do. Occasionally during deliverance Holy Spirit would open my spiritual eyes, and I could see what others could not. At other times, the Holy Spirit would allow me to sense what to do based on my body symptoms like pressure, more specifically, in my hands. Finally, He began to give me utterance. During these times, I could not see or discern, but I could hear. All of these realizations are personal experiences. The problem lies with people promoting personal understanding above faith, scriptures, the Holy Spirit, and God's kingdom (Luke 11:20). My previous training was gift-based. But now, it is based on kingdom understanding and governmental positioning. In other words, less "personal ideas" and more God-centered work.

## Deliverance for the Prophet First

Official prophets and prophetic people should desire to set the captives free as Jesus did (Isaiah 61:1, Luke 4:18). We have confidence in God as the master deliverer. One requirement is not to be contaminated by the past. Our past has a way of becoming acquainted with our future. It comes to settle debts with all victims – young, old, smart, famous, talented, anointed, gifted, etc. And wounds are the most common forms of payment.

Remember the author section? In it, I talked about my two experiences and why I turned my devotion to Yahweh. My prophetic duties and disciplines would prove whether I had truly learned lessons from my previous experience. "A Prophet's mandate exceeds the practice of uttering a predictive prophecy. It includes the balancing criteria that apply wisdom, knowledge, insight, character, and integrity to the predictions. They refer to the inner governance that provides the checks and balances that restrain a prophet's natural and carnal proclivities. It also inspires the messenger to choose the higher and God-glorifying path of prophetic service. Finally, questions of ethics and morality come to light in developing sound prophetic disciplines. The disciplined prophet assures correctness and guards against prophetic perversion and seduction" (The Prophet's Dictionary no. 1120 pg.419).

After much prayer, fasting, and scripture study, I was choosing the restraints of the mantle. Prophets have a responsibility to guard the office and their station.

## Chapter 4 Deliverance

### PART 2

### Systems and Cycles

Understanding how cycles and triggers work can help address misconceptions about learned behavior. But accomplishing this means facing difficulties differently. Normalizing unhealthy behavior builds unprosperous cycles that cause damage to our mental and spiritual processes. To challenge those chaotic cycles, we look to the learning process.

Most Christians accept the idea that life and behaviors change without putting in any effort. However, this is not accurate. Yes, accepting Christ brings immediate changes concerning adoption and fidelities. However, producing new things in life only happen by gathering information and renewing the mind. Therefore, practicing the mind of Christ in every area of life means reducing ungodly influences and ignorant thinking. Family life, financial life, academic life, spiritual life, career life, social life, and health and wellness need annual review. The problem is being aware of inefficient life processes versus changing unproductive behavior. These are two different things. To know means to comprehend. Most believers know in theory. The bible says in 2 Peter 1:3, "His divine power has given us everything we need for life and godliness through the knowledge of Him who called us by His own glory and excellence." All things pertaining to life and godliness through knowledge are keys to life. Godliness means piety. Helps word studies says, "Someone's inner response to the things of God which show itself in godly reverence." Life is in God, but more than that. Life is what we do for God while we are still breathing.

Notice that some influential people of God are only powerful spiritually. Then, others are powerful in business or finances. Few people function as a whole and powerful human being in all capacities of life. Limited information, out-of-order strategy, or dysfunctional mental processes are reasons for varying results. Contemplating a new way of living is one thing, but to souly overthrow false legislative effects, take discipline. The bible says, "For we wrestle not against flesh and blood" (Eph. 6:12). Thayer's Greek Lexicon says wrestle is from *ballo,* meaning to vibrate, shake. Our enemy wants to shake us mentally and spiritually to distract our focus. He knows that both areas produce a full Christ-centered life.

Wrestling is a contest in which each endeavor to throw the other. However, in this case, we are wrestling with our thoughts, including the projections of others, ungodly beliefs, social consciousness, and so much more. To wrestle also means to be focused, intentional, and strategic. The physically strong does not necessarily have enough strength to win against a focused, deliberate, and strategic person. If a physically weaker individual has enough information about their opponent - they will win! If we do the same with our thinking, we will win too! Nevertheless, an indecisive person will work on one thing today and something else tomorrow. He or she will never come out as a winner because of distractions.

Diversion is the oldest trick in the book because it promotes inconsistency, causing a prophet to change focus. Our enemy has studied our traits, cycles, and pressure points. He then waits patiently, watching for old patterns to reset. Afterward, he reenters our life and starts his attack like in times past. But, Jesus crushed Satan and the systems he uses to entrap humanity. Luke 4:18 says, "The Spirit of the Lord is on me because He has anointed me to preach the gospel to the poor; He sent me to heal the brokenhearted, to proclaim liberty to the captives, and recovery of sight to the blind, to set at liberty those under oppression." A few things to look at here. One, the anointing to preach yields deliverance. It debunks the theory that anyone can preach the gospel. Context is important. So let's look at the Great Commission. Mark 16:14-17 says, "Jesus appeared to the eleven and rebuked them for their unbelief and hardness of heart. Because they did not believe those who saw Him after He rose, he said to them, "Go into all the world and preach the gospel to every creature. And these signs will accompany those who believe: in My name, they will drive out demons; they will speak in new tongues; they will pick up snakes with their hands, and if they drink poison, it will not harm them; they will lay hands on the sick, and they will be well." Who was Christ speaking to? After Christ appeared, did they believe? Did signs follow them? Before you preach the gospel, ask yourself, do I meet the qualifications of the Great Commission? Am I zealous, or am I sent? After I preach, will my life confuse a new convert about holiness and truth? Do my social media posts have an underlying tone of secularism or compromise? Preaching the gospel is about the Lord working with you (Mark 16:20). It is not about you working for yourself.

The gospel also confronts poverty. Healing for the heart is added to the list, and freedom for prisoners of war or captives. Finally, the gospel restores physical and mental blindness (G5185). Again, the Lord demonstrated deliverance because he prepared (give or take 15-17 years of training), God appointed him (after John the Baptist baptized him), and Holy Spirit anointed Jesus. "For we wrestle not against flesh and blood, but against principalities, powers, rulers of darkness of this world, against spiritual wickedness in high places" (Ephesian 6:12). We cannot preach "effectively" without the enforcement of God's kingdom backing us. A few categories sum up the systems regulated by Satan. Principalities, powers, rulers of darkness, and spiritual wickedness in high places. Through organizational efficiency, Satan creates barricades that frustrate godly outcomes. The Holy Spirit, the anointings, and the gospel are the greatest weapons against Satan and his falsehood. God appointed Jesus in Luke 4:18, which legalized him to confront and abolish the powers that captured society through sin. Therefore Jesus is deliverance!

Deliverance is a kingdom system founded on salvation and Christ. Today, the most used form of salvation is in Roman 9:10. However, systematic structure governed by principalities, powers, rulers of darkness, and spiritual wickedness in the heavenly realms regulate the world's economies affecting its citizen. In the O.T., people needed deliverance from evil enemies, and nations needed help defending themselves from adversaries. King Saul is one of those people. He wanted help from an evil spirit. 1 Samuel 16:14 - 23 explains that the Lord's Spirit left Saul, and a tormenting one replaced him. Saul needed deliverance. The bible says an anointed and skilled young man helped Saul.

The necessities of confronting evil spirits in this case are:
1. Anointing
2. Holy Spirit
3. Skill

Saul's servant recommended David because he was skillful. Secondly, the Spirit of the Lord was with him, and the anointing. In this instance, deliverance came through the three things above.
David was involved in another act of deliverance when he faced Goliath. Saul and his army were at a deadlock with their adversaries. Nevertheless, the Lord, along with a skillful David, killed Goliath. Both situations required assistance from an invisible kingdom. Most times, the method used in deliverance is scriptures. However, alternate methods can help a tormented soul too. Other formulas for salvation include destroying systems. What skill will work within an organized structure to deliver a neighborhood, school, family, or nation? The Old Testament has stories about people who opposed systems. Abraham, Noah, Moses, Joseph, and many others are known for deliverance. They had three things in common, the anointing, the Holy Spirit or Spirit of the Lord, and a skill.

Some skills are spiritual, but the Holy Spirit helps us utilize them in a way that confronts issues and provides a service. Men and women featured in the Old Testament transported people from captivity to freedom by using governmental resources from an unseen kingdom ruled by the Lord. His world is in the invisible spheres. However, it is visible to those who learn the secrets of His systems.

Notice that Hebrews 4:18 and 1 Samuel 16:23 use the terms come on, or upon to explain import, export, and connections. Prophets connect, then exporting occurs after Yahweh imports or supply him or her with a resource (the anointing). Understand that we have witnessed exporting without connection with many prophets. Prophets have a gift and calling. However, working the gift or faculty without the call is problematic. The question is who and what are they called to? Gifting in the kingdom is a resource, and it comes without repentance (Romans 11:29). The difference between a God-connected prophet and a gifted prophet is the Holy Spirit. The Holy Spirit is a God-head member. He powers the kingdom of Yahweh. The demonstration of a gift in a person may not suggest belonging to the nation of the Lord Jesus Christ. Who authorized the prophet? Whoever licenses a prophet becomes the support system for his or her exporting. Prophets demonstrate authority and power for a kingdom and source. Re-examining the text shows the ability to represent the kingdom through networking. Nevertheless, no connection conveys exporting illegally or without credentials.

1 John 3:8-10 explains the connection through procreation. It says, "For this purpose was the Son of God manifested that He might destroy the works of the

devil: whoever is born of Yahweh doth not sin because he is born of God. In this, the children of God are manifest, and the children of the devil: whosoever doeth not righteousness is not of Him, neither he that loveth not his brother." Prophets are born prophets. So, separating the authorized and unauthorized is a matter of connection.

Both kingdoms have offspring, but the difference between them is sin. One group despises sin, embraces righteousness, and loves his brothers. The other group is like Cain, a hater, and murder. Verse fifteen says whosoever hates his brother is a murderer, and ye know that no murderer has eternal life abiding in him. Prophets who hate others divide and murder the people around their sphere. In my Haitian culture, there are women called prophetess who practice voodoo. People respect these women back home and in the states. Though women are not the only practicing priestess in Haiti, I use them as an example because they are called prophetesses. Although people revere them as prophetesses, they do not represent Elohim, and their export is on behalf of another. On the other hand, our challenge is the church prophets who hate, murder and sin. Who are they exporting for, and are they the offspring of the Lord?

### Deliverance: New Birth

For what purpose do prophets export? Identifying our works will determine which kingdom we belong to. Rebirth is the only way to receive a new heart and spirit. Ezekiel 36:26 says, "A new heart (3820 *leb*) will I give you, and a new spirit (7307 *ruach*) I will put in you. I will take away the stony heart out of your flesh, and I will give you a heart of flesh" (parenthesis added). The new birth comes equipped with a new *leb*, which translates as the inner man (Bible Hub, H3820). Furthermore, the new *ruach* means breath, wind, and spirit (Bible Hub, H7307). God sanctified the people, both outwardly and inwardly. Next, God gave them a bonus. He said, "I put My Ruach *within you* (7130 *qereb*) and cause you to walk in My statutes. You will be careful to observe My ordinances." Yahweh's Spirit was positioned, specifically in the *qereb* (inward part or midst), to influence the *leb* and *ruach*. Our God delivered Israel from old systems and their influences, for His name's sake. He made Israel new. Notice that *satoria* (G4991) happened before the birth, death, and resurrection of Christ. Ladies and gentlemen, deliverance rests on our access to the Kingdom of God and our ability to export it. Exporting kingdom goods refutes darkness, and it empowers the prophet to engage in warfare without fear.

## Fear and Deliverance

Prophets who fear warfare or deliverance should never engage in such activities. There are many reasons for this, but disloyalty and torment are the main two. Fear forces a prophet to overcompensate by exaggerating, projecting, or deflecting. In Pigs in the Parlor, the author explains why fear provides an opening for evil spirits (Hammond, pg. 95). Fearful prophets are usually unprocessed in faith areas, meaning he or she failed foundational lessons. Deliverance is not a game, nor is it for a novice. It involves kingdom against kingdom. Moreover, long before times of warfare, God convinces a prophet of who he is. Apostle Joshua Selman says, "When a demon fortifies a mindset, the mindset becomes a doorway into a person's life. Afterward, their thoughts become influenced by demon spirits to ensure repetition" (This Is How-to Pull-Down Strongholds, Selman). Apostle Selman believes that mindsets are gates and doors in the spirit realm. He says, "They can authorize the entrance of the Word of God and other things of the kingdom." If this is true, a prophet who is fearful of deliverance will be vulnerable against the powers of darkness operating through a person. For this reason, wavering cannot be present. Use Matthew 9:25, Mark 5:40, and Luke 8:54 as premises.

## Difference Between Control and Discipline

Unlike control, discipline promotes consistency. If a person, regardless of title or position, is forced by another to engage in spiritual warfare, they can become overwhelmed by anxiety, possibly sabotaging the entire deliverance session. Carefully preparing for deliverance is the best approach. Take care to resist the temptation to control people and situations. Mainly because a spirit of control breeds timidity, causing people to be afraid of judgment or punishment. Pay close attention to signs of unhealthy competitiveness, perfection, and affectation. It is a good indicator of the first stages of fear. Here is an example: if parents or caretakers fear losing control, they may exert dominance, triggering intimidation in their children and creating an environment that promotes insecurity and regret, which are tools of darkness. Overly self-conscious children grow into adults who are prone to people-pleasing. Though this is not always the case, controlling environments are unhealthy. Therefore, recycling dysfunction is a normal response to learned behavior. Finally, control smothers and vexes the Holy Spirit. It also puts out the fire of the Holy Ghost in a believer. Soon people become powerless with robotic mannerisms that follow only the instructions of people and not the Lord, God. Queen Jezebel is an excellent example of control and fear. Any operation that accommodates the personalities or characteristics of

Jezebel becomes an inroad for control and micromanaging.

## Deliverance: Tolerance and Sin

Tolerance is another dysfunction because what we tolerance grows, develops, and shapes into matured fruit. Eventually, changes are noticeable, and the standards and convictions they once held diminish. Satan gave Eve another idea because she tolerated his company and suggestions. Soon he darkened her understanding of truth with deception (2 Corinthians 3:14). Remember this: whatever we tolerate will replicate among us and the population.

The word says light shines in the darkness (John 1:5). The only way to get rid of an ungodly influence is with the truth. Jesus is the light of men. Life was in him, and his life was the light of men (v.4). Light and darkness are always at war. When believers tolerate any form of darkness, the lesser light begins to rule. God has made two great lights - the essential light to govern the day and the lesser light to govern the night. What business does lesser light have ruling over God's more perfect light in us? It is not a matter of not loving people, but people are not loving God. "God loves the world that He gave his only begotten son so that whoever believes shall not perish but have eternal life" (John 3:15). What do we believe?

There was a time when the inhabitants of the earth were at a vast disadvantage. So, God sent his only son as ransom for whoever would receive him. He allowed believers to become born-again. God understands the power of sin and death. He wanted to save humanity from its infection. Those who willingly sin carry a deadly seed. The Bible says, "Therefore to him, that knows to do good, and doeth [it] not, to him, it is, sin (James 4:17)." Sin and death entered the world through one man - Adam (Romans 5:12-21). However, our Father granted propitiations for the plague that takes the life of humanity. Sin and death should not be comfortable enough to enter the house of the Lord and stay there. Sin only remains in a place because of tolerance. I know that churchdom may frown upon some of the past practices of the Bible. But how do we stop the plague in God's house?

First, confront the sin. Give him or her an opportunity to choose Godly counsel, deliverance, or even nothing at all. It is their right to decide. God never imposes His will upon us. Because of this, we should not override people's decisions either. However, put protocols in place for when a worker, minister, pastor, or prophet falls into habitual sin. Secondly, have a plan b—a person who can fill in. Leaders tolerate immorality sometimes because they need people working in the church building. Our need for musicians, singers, sound engineers, and the like make us partial. However, our Father is not biased. I like what Billy Graham said, "God is intolerant of sin but tolerant of the sinner." He said to the woman in John 8:11, "I neither condemn thee go and sin no more." He forgave her because he loved her. Nevertheless, he condemned her sin because he loathed it with a Holy hatred (Graham). The third step is to restore them. Shepherds and leaders need systems of recovery. Forgetting to restore a person gives the enemy an advantage of winning people back to the kingdom of Satan.

## Having A Consistent Mentality

Discipline involves a person's will and their right to choose. More than that, a new system can develop in place of the old. Eventually, discipline yields a fruit called self-control (Galatians 5:22). To engage darkness, one must be free of elemental sin especially, unforgiveness, control, fear, manipulation, rejection, and double-mindedness. If prophets do not renew their minds, they become casualties of war or double agents. The art of war insists that all warriors or defenders commit to the desired outcome.

One of the first rules of action is to know your enemy. Afterward, dedication and having a consistent mentality is also necessary. James 1:7 warns of doublemindedness, saying that wavering is like a wave driven by winds with no direction. These are the manifestations of a double-minded person. A double-minded person is unstable, while people with a strong sense of self-control become disciplined ones. God needs disciplined people to engage the evil systems of darkness. Whether we realize it or not, whatever we do consistently develops a mindset. The mindset creates a process, and the process affects our perception, and perception leads to behavior. So, actions prove our conviction, mental process, and attitude. Therefore, to win against evil powers is to recruit those who allow the Holy Spirit to develop the fruit of self-control.

## Problematic Prophets/Ministers

Today, some of us are witnessing the rapid emergence of prophets all over the globe. Nevertheless, the alarming thing is that they are accurate, precise men and women of God with mental, emotional, and spiritual wounds. In other words, these prophetic people are gifted but not healed or processed.

Typically, prophets have undergone a series of refusal, bullying, lack of emotional support, disowning, isolation, parental abandonment, and the list continues. These emotional wounds are access points for demonic harassment and tormenting. The best way for a prophet to become mature is the same way that babes or novices in Christianity do. Through study, diligence, trials, mentorship, processing, prayer, learning about faith, obedience to God, and learning about God and his attributes. Deliverance is a big part of our processing. So, be patient with yourself. You are recovering a part of who you are.

## Chapter 5 SYMBOLISM, THE PROPHETIC & PROPHETS

The symbolism of the prophetic and prophets all coexist for communication purposes. Symbols are images used to represent other things or express intangible or cryptic ideas (The Prophet's Dictionary no 1481 pg. 548). Similarly, it stands for something else, especially a material object representing something abstract. Learning from the perspective of research and studies builds knowledge. However, symbolism is a part of the prophetic sphere. God reveals and confirms revelation and additional ideas, themes, and wonders by this medium. Throughout history, Biblical themes measured symbolism. The book of Daniel is replete with codification. One example is Daniel 5, the mysterious hand and the writing on the wall. Notice that King Belshazzar called enchanters, the Chaldeans, and the conjurers, but no one could interpret the meaning of Mene, Mene, Tekel, and Parsin. Symbols need interpretation. Therefore, the vessel (person) and its source determine interpretation, misinterpretation, or perplexity.

Though prophets have access to the prophetic dimension, their connection to Yahweh is paramount to ensure accuracy. The Chaldean's were master trackers; groomed to articulate the mystical. They tracked based on numbers and signs; they were astrologers (H3779. Kasday). Astrology now includes horoscopes, tarot readings, and other crafts. It is called pseudoscience in mainstream circles. However, even today, Chaldean's are recognized as the second-century founders of astrology. Yet, God created numbers, meanings, and symbolism. Again, interpretation exists based on the origin of authority. Prophets are professionals, and to err is human. But the precision of a prophet reflects the skill and accuracy identical to the Chaldeans. However, the prophet exists to comply with the prophetic office and not merely execution. So, what separates the two agents?

The Chaldeans and prophets are like instruments or tools. Therefore, knowing who uses the agent is vital because the adversary has tools too. The tribe of Issachar and the Chaldeans are also similar, except one practiced astronomy and the other astrology. Studying the cosmos is not criminal. However, how they procure knowledge brings about critical distinctions. The Chaldean and other craft workers worked from the dark side of the spiritual realms known as the kingdom of darkness or the demonic spheres. Colossian 1:13 says, "He has rescued us from the domain of darkness and transferred us to the kingdom of his beloved son." (Berean Study Bible). There are mysteries about light and darkness that operate in the spirit world. God is the progenitor of light and truth. While charming and bewitchment align with dark-works, and Satan is its source. The symbolism in Daniel 5 came from a source that the Chaldeans did not know, causing perplexion rather than cognizance. Therefore, they could not interpret the writing from God. Demons or devils who live in the second heavens will not penetrate God's revelatory realms. Firstly, the protocols in heaven will not permit it. Secondly, darkness cannot exist in light, literally and spiritually. Magicians are bound to their realms of knowledge because their power source or deity is uninformed of heaven's intelligence.

The authority of a prophet should not rely merely on gifts or predictions. He or she must connect to the source of light, who is God with his Holy Spirit, through the rebirth in Christ. Remember that the driving points of anything in the spirit world depend on who authors the information.

### Symbolism: Dreams & Visions

Dreams and visions contain symbolism. But the interpretation of these is also based on sources. God-inspired, demonically influenced, and personal visualization all have roots in the otherworldly. When a dreamer goes to sleep, he/she enters another plane mentally or spiritually. Their dreams can be literal or symbolic. The dreamer is not in control of their night visions. Many factors influence what a dreamer sees when asleep. However, all dreams do not originate in God, but he gives humans messages in their dreams, including warning, prediction, instructions, and many other directives. Dreams within another dream are multifaceted and even troublesome but, decoding happens through our connection. If you remember, I was transparent about how a person misinterpreted the night-vision that the Lord gave me. Those unfortunate events would not have happened if I connected to my source.

The adversary creates scenarios as well. He uses people to intercept dreamers in the dream state to entrap or project falseness. Water dreams, sexual dreams, and other persuasions manipulate the dreamer into many things. "Then thou scares me with dreams and terrifies me through visions: so that my soul chooses strangulation and death rather than life" (Job 7:14 - 15). If the adversary can influence people with fear, paranoia, panic, or sleep paralysis, he is pleased. According to the Journal of Personality and Social Psychology (Vol. 96, No. 2), dreams influence people's decisions and attitudes. Terrifying dreams could make one anxious or nervous. And stealing the confidence of a prophet could chip away at his or her faith. Furthermore, without faith, it is impossible to please God (Hebrews 11:6), and he or she will not prophesy (Romans 12:6).

House prophets and additional ecclesial mantles carry the tools to help people experiencing such warfare. House prophets use revelation accessed from the prophetic dimensions and the word of the Lord as a barricade. The prophetic defuses the diabolical intentions, plans, or traps of the adversary. Prophets easily reach these spheres through training and governmental access, but mainly through Holy Spirit (Acts 1:8). House prophets guard the gates of a local temple, and they work with the Shamar to cover the pastor, staff, and congregants. The soul of the house prophet and Shamar should not tarnish or compromise Godly people or official assignments. Instead, the guardianship aptly developed in a prophet pushes them into warfare mode when torment or affliction troubles anyone in their care. Prophets understand 2 Corinthians 10:4-5, "The weapons we fight with are not the weapons of this world. On the contrary, they have divine power to demolish strongholds. We demolish arguments and every pretension that sets itself up against the knowledge of God. We take captive every thought to make it obedient to Christ" (English Standard Version).

### The Prophetic

The prophetic is the predictive sphere of supernatural communications (The Prophet's Dictionary). Meaning anyone can access these spheres if they have a connection. Supernatural communication goes beyond natural resources. Think about it this way, anyone who has money or good credit can purchase a new phone. But, if they do not have a phone carrier to connect with, they only have a new phone. On the other hand, phone numbers connect us to people and places. But, if you don't have a person's phone number, you will find another way to connect. Supernatural communication means that people are connecting to the spirit world. But who are they connecting with?

The ministry work of a prophet involves supernatural communication. The prophet and prophetic types embrace the disciplines and practices of revelatory ministry that come from these spheres and reflect the skills, abilities, and resources that facilitate the prophet's ministry and fundamentally empowers the mantle. Understand that the prophet's spirit comes manufactured and coded for the prophetic spheres. However, the prophet mantle is the spiritual garment authorized by its author or founder and works as a toolbox for the user or wearer.

Prophets have a prophetic measure that aptly corresponds with the mantle, the ward, or the directive. Therefore, the occupation of holy prophets is to do God's work. So prophesying is not the principal function of the office. For instance, the governor's office includes giving speeches to peers and the public. However, it is not the primary description of what they do. God employs his prophets based on trustworthiness, while others deploy based on gifts and ability. Some prophets have the power to perform but are not empowered to withstand the agency of Satan. Selah.

The guardianship, governance, and guidance of the prophets cannot be to the people first. Loyalty to Christ fuels the genuine service prophets performs for people. However, twisted devotedness provokes the uprise of occultic tendencies in the churches of God. Therefore, we see the resignation of a powerless church demanding recognition without God's kingdom's backing. The bride or Ekklesia of Christ can be charismatic, and priest-prophets do well in refocusing the Godly institutions.

### Prophets

Prophets are born prophets. But, seeing, hearing, dreaming, and discernment are activities. Therefore, undisciplined prophets carry God's gift, regardless of their character or inability to access the pure prophetic spheres. Undisciplined prophets speak presumptuously and have no spiritual regimen. They only know or understand the spirit world from experience, promoting powerlessness for Christ while masquerading as Christ's representatives. Others choose the dark side of life, admittedly denying Christ and his salvation for the earthy rewards that do not remain. These are the modern-day wizards, white lighters, witches, crafters, voodoo priests, channelers, Yogini, palm readers, psychics, etc.

When prophets use "fallen" information to predict the Lord's word, erroneous patterns begin. Traditional theology and religious thinkers box God into concepts. However, the same is true of those who super-spiritualize based on ideas. Balanced prophetic teaching establishes guidelines for trying prophecy and testing those who say that they are prophets. The prophetic sphere requires competence to hear and see God, even as he speaks through other modes. These prophets understand the foundational prerequisite for prophetic manifestation. The prophetic sphere is like a communication base that sends signals, messages, and agents (angelic delegates) back and forth to creation. All of the above starts with the prophet's spirit However, it ends with the ascension to the official measure of the office to which the prophet will sit. Legal ascension happens through a relationship with Christ, and faithfulness to God and his kingdom, while allowing the fruit of the Spirit to mature. Elijah's ascension in the chariot is an example of a legal rise.

Yahweh starts the process of election by calling a prophet through dreams. Next, he seeks to restore the prophet's soul while teaching them the premise of soul restoration (Luke 21:19). While training the prophet, many relationships are challenged. Finally, true surrender happens through multiple trials and testing, resculpting the mind, will, and emotions. The order in which these things happen is genuinely up to the Lord. However, one thing is for sure God's process makes the prophet eligible for office. Most people think that

God forces prophets into duty. However, this is not the case. Your mind might be thinking about Joah right now. Well, even though God caused the extenuating circumstances, Joah changed his mind (Jonah 2:1-2). Once Joah realized that kingdom duty was more important than death. He changed his mind quickly. God chose Joah, but Joah needed to choose God. Joah's story is famous in the Christian world. But have you ever heard a preacher say that God wanted another yes from Joah? Joah knew God, but he was stubborn about his kingdom assignment. Prophets can choose to be on official duty or to sit on the sidelines and be normal. Usually, this is a soul issue and not a God issue.

One way we take possession of our soul is to acknowledge what affects or afflicts our emotions. Emotions are a crucial indicator of many things. They tell us if we have a propensity to lean towards sadness or anger. Maybe, you or someone like you goes through life emotionless. What are your emotions revealing about the condition of your soul? Let us engage in an activity in the next chapter.

# 6 Soul of the Prophet

## Soul of the Prophet

The soul of a prophet is the canvas of his or her perception. A famous scripture is 3 John 1:2, "Beloved, I wish above all things that you may prosper and be in health, even as your soul prospers." Two words to look at are prosper and soul. The Greek word for prosper is *euodoo*: "to have a prosperous journey. Its usage is to cause to prosper and pass. Therefore, I have a happy, successful journey. Hence I prosper." Prosperity is not confined to finance or assets. The condition of a prophet's soul thrives on maturity and mental health.

Although mental health is essential, sanctification and holiness heal the soul, too (2 Timothy 2:21 KJV). The bible says, "And the very God of peace sanctify you wholly, and your whole spirit and soul and body be preserved blameless until the coming of Christ" (1

Thess. 5:23 KJV). Our soul needs the sanctification of Christ living in us. Keeping God's laws does not happen through willpower alone. However, we escape corruption by our partnership with Christ and the knowledge of God (2 Peter 1:2-4). How we journey through life is not the issue. How we overcome is the life-force behind a prosperous soul. People grow physically. However, can onlookers observe brokenness in the behavior or speech of the prophet? Is he or she successfully thriving in multiple areas of life (not just spiritually or prophetically)? Can you witness prosperity on and off the pulpit? How do others speak of him or her? Looking at a prophet's resume will not prove anything but accomplishments. Look beyond the outward display and discover what posture he or she continually displays. Then you will find the motive and character of that prophet.

As an individual, it is essential to understand that your distinct personality developed over time. You are you because of a variety of influences. Your perspective is by what you experienced from an incredibly early age. However, it is the prophet's responsibility to possess or govern his or her soul. Luke 21:19 says, "By patient endurance, you will gain your soul." To the persons who rehearse disadvantages, failures, or hardships – it is time to take possession of your soul. If you are wondering how to start, look no further. The following pages contain questions that can gauge what you think about and the emotions that accompany them.

Answer the following questions.
**Activity:**

1. In the past 24 hours, what emotion did you express the most (e.g. sad, hopeless, concerned, excited, angry, happy, etc.)?

   _____
   _____

2. Did you feel like your emotions were out of your control? If yes, on a scale from 1 – 10, how out of control did you feel?

   _____
   _____

3. Do your emotions tend to be unpredictable, or do you find your feelings are calm and thought-out?

   _____
   _____

4. Finally, how do others feel about your display of emotions? Do they say things like, "That's why I don't talk to you because you're too emotional" or "Why do you have to control everything?" Maybe an example might be, "You're so easy to talk to." "You're a great boss or friend."

   _____
   _____

5. If you could change anything about your emotional responses, what would you change?

_____

_____

6. What step are you open to exploring?

_____

_____

No matter what your answers are. You just estimated where your emotions are. Now, you can begin to make necessary changes for the betterment of your soul. Here is the truth of the matter. If you do not know where you are, then how can you gauge where you are going? In Luke 21:19, the author explains the hardship of being a believer. Jesus' reasoning behind Luke 21:10-19 was to instruct believers on:

- What persecution is, and the inevitability of persecution because of Christ?
- He assures us that he will deal with our rival.
- Knowing that you are hated, and still have confidence that the world will not harm you.

After he teaches his points, Jesus says, "By your patience, possess your soul." After you endure pain, separation, betrayal, and even murder use your right to decide. Do not lose your faith or your sanity while going through life. Find help for your soul.

## Chapter 7 Abuse Of Power

### Part 1

### Honor vs. False Honor

Be careful not to call control honor. Honor is mutual, like shaking someone's hand. Both individuals put forth an effort to reach out and grasp hands. The same is true when we honor God. We return our respect with a posture of gratitude. An excellent example of honor is when a soldier receives a commendation for heroism. The United States honors the soldier because of his actions for his country and team. He or she trained physically and mentally, passed tests, and the government deployed them into combat. During the war, the soldier did something honorable. So, they are well deserving of a commendation. Real honor is always mutual.

In the bible, we read, "Children obey your parents in the Lord: for this is right. Honor thy father and mother; which is the first commandment with promise; that it may be well with thee and you live long on the earth. And fathers provoke not your children to wrath: but bring them up in the nurture and admonition of the Lord" (Ephesian 6:1-4). Most people focus on the first portion of this scripture, but God's full thought is mutual honor. The father has a responsibility not to vex, irritate or provoke his kid. He is also responsible for nurturing his children's idea of the Lord. If children are not obeying at the early childhood age, either the parent is not planting and cultivating the seed of honor, or the children are watching behavior and patterns versus hearing instructions. Parents are the first representatives of God that children observe. And parents should exhibit godly behavior. According to the social learning theory, children learn by observation. Therefore, the child at toddlerhood absorbs the elements in the environment. Fathers who model Christ teach their children integrity, safety, love, and other unspoken principles. Today, most children do not model their parents. They model the most significant influencer around them (cartoons, YouTube influencers, characters, etc.).

## "Godly Honor

"Turn, on backsliding children, saith the Lord, for I am married to you" (Jer. 3:14). This scripture is an example of parental efforts towards children. Our most outstanding example of good parenting comes from Abba-Father. He continuously reaches to his children to redeem us and call us home to salvation in Christ. It is because he honors covenant. We find that God remains faithful to humanity, even though history proves our unfaithfulness to Him. Scripture says to be devoted to one another in love. Moreover, "To honor one another above ourselves" (Romans 12:10). 1 Timothy 5:17 recommends double honor to the elder who directs the affairs of the church. In these scriptures, honor is time. It means to fix the value and to price. Its usages are (a) I value at a price or estimate. (b) I honor or reverence. We assign esteem or preciousness to one another. So mutual honor is a choice that is reflected in our efforts.

## What is In Identity?

False honor changes a prophet's identity. Our identity develops based on who parents us. In most cases, prophets need to understand Elohim as a father before they can trust and serve Him. Broken or false identity conceals our authentic self. It usually misleads and alters the perception of others based on what has been presented. Charm, eagerness, eloquence, and even silence are personas that cover real character. A prophet may not know that they lack self-awareness. Broken identity stresses detachment from others, causing social isolation to hide from fear, disappointment, and rejection. Short-term friendships, multiple connections, but few relationships are breeding grounds for depression or self-exaltation. Discovering that they associate best when utilizing their gift convinces the prophet that a genuine friendship or other connection is about their ability to give the word of the Lord. However, most times, it is not the Lord's word. It is a word to convince or sway others for acceptance, fueling an emotional connection rather than a balanced inter-relational connection. Everyone is not a destiny helper or sent to help with ministry endeavors. These thoughts lead to ego trips, high-mindedness, and variance—seeing people as less than or as bartering objects fosters a controlling and even dark persona.

Satan is the master of all things dark, including a false or counterfeit appearance. His debut in the Garden of Eden confirms his ability to deceive. When prophets display deceptive characteristics, their ministry and integrity are in jeopardy. Deception is not a behavior that one takes on overnight. It encompasses patterns from childhood that relates to envy, insecurity, and anger. But, before this, lying or storytelling becomes a pattern. Afterward, poor habits form, and sooner or later, covetousness develops. To deal with these personality defaults, engage in prayer, become self-aware, and choose Godly council. Most importantly, scriptural study and intentionality help a prophet develop a good character. The fruit of the Spirit is a good indicator that a Christian believer is on the right track for a prophetic ministry. If a prophet neglects repentance, sanctification, or relationship with Christ, and discipleship, he or she finds ways to relieve their emotional and mental stressors. It is called a coping mechanism.

## False Honor and Theft

False honor can also produce a con artist persona (Leviticus 19:11). Con artists are thieves who use charisma rather than muscle. They learn how to blend in to go unnoticed by security guards and cops. Usually, closed off from their emotions, he or she sometimes seem emotionless. Their calm deminer can fool others into believing that they are reserved and even poised. But the truth is, people never see their real persona, which can pull people in as loyalists. These prophets use people without proper compensation (Deuteronomy 24:14-15; Leviticus 19:13). Prophets can steal by manipulating others, which is a sin in both the kingdom of heaven and earth. Scammers call thousands of numbers a day in hopes of defrauding people out of confidential information or their money. They misrepresent the phone or electric company to get banking information. Others offer people opportunities of gaining more income, and their most targeted victims are the elderly. Some prophets do the same thing. They have a way of manipulating people out of their resources with prophetic words. Abuse of power happens on many levels.

The best way to reciprocate honor is to value people. And remember to respect their sacrifice and funding. The church runs on donations, volunteers, and community support. So, disregarding that is a direct indication of misguided ministry directives or lack of accountability. Either way, the misappropriation of power is inevitable. When a prophet craves validation, that is a crucial indicator that they are not ready for power or influence. The benefits of being a prophet will always hinder their moral boundary. It is why our identity is the main thing that affects our use of power. Abuse of power is usually a sign of broken or false identity.

## Identity Theft

Identity theft is a growing market in the world today. Some people refer to the dark web as the most resourceful place to steal someone's identity. Most people use agencies to prevent identity theft, including cybersecurity. Prophets who assume someone's identity to draw crowds and followers are fraudulent. Attracting crowds is not the problem since Jesus often attracted crowds of people. However, changing our personality to fit something that we are not is problematic. Jesus understood that his assignments would lead him to his ultimate purpose of the cross. Jesus was assignment-driven, and that led to the authenticity of his followers and following. Even when the rich ruler wanted to follow him, Jesus knew the young man's heart and resisted his offer (Luke 18:18-30). Saying 'good teacher' was the ruler's attempt at flattery. Jesus responds, "Why do you call me good?" In other words, what is your motive? During his time, Jesus touched the lives of many. However, he trained the twelve people assigned to him. Jesus did not think about numbers or how many towns to hit in a month for an offering. No, he focused on his mission. Many people lose time collecting money and people. But if a prophet spends time on unfruitful works, then how do they recover God's people?

### Navigate Through

To navigate beyond abusive power, become well-rounded. Education is a great tool. Whether you are interested in a Christian facility or a regular university, go and learn. Maybe college is not for you. There are certificate programs that are great as well. Learning new things, challenging yourself, and connecting to others who are not your subordinate helps personal development. You learn to ask for help. You remember the benefits of community, especially in group projects. What is fun to you? And how often do you make time to do it? Having fun and enjoying life is a beneficial way to stimulate socialization (Ecclesiastes 3:13;

Ecclesiastes 5:18-20). Socializing outside of church activities is a great way to connect with believers and unbelievers. Pottery classes, book clubs, skating rinks are fantastic choices to enjoy life. Most times, abusing power is all about controlling people and environments. But, when we socialize, we see ourselves better, including the good, the bad, and the ugly. We can choose to submit those flaws to Abba and become better rather than trying to control the narrative of how others act and communicate.

## Codependency

Prophets can tell if they are codependent through socializing. Codependency is a learned behavior that usually stems from past behavioral patterns and emotional difficulties (What to Know About Codependent Relationships by Jennifer Berry). We view codependency in two ways. A caretaker is necessary for a disabled or senior person. Likewise, children are naturally dependent on guardians or parents for financial, emotional, or other support. "Codependency is more than clinginess. It represents one-sidedness with a person who needs to be needed" (Medical News Today, Berry). Usually, they neglect responsibilities for their person of interest. They abandon other relationships to convince their enabler of commitment and security. Codependent relationships can be among friends, romantic partners, or family members. Friends and family of a codependent person may recognize that something is

wrong. Codependency is an emotional or mental health issue, and the symptoms of codependency include:
- There is no satisfaction in things done in life other than doing something for a person.
- They are staying in a relationship even though your partner does hurtful things.
- Does anything to please their enabler no matter what the expense to themselves?
- Uses all their time and energy to give their partner everything that they ask for.
- Feel guilty about thinking of themselves in the relationship and will not express any personal needs or desire.
- Ignore their morals or consciousness to do what the other person wants.
- They feel constant anxiety about their relationship due to their passion for making the other person happy.

When identity centers around another person, unhealthy biases are inevitable, creating unbeneficial soul ties. Saying no becomes difficult if the prophet deals with inadequacy, guilt, and perfectionism. These underlining issues make for power struggles and poor communication skills, making things worst for a person who wants to heal from co-dependency.

## Soul Ties

A soul tie is when souls knit together. Becoming one flesh is the act of sealing the deal (Mark 10:7-9). The scripture says, "Man will leave his father and mother and be joined to his wife, and the two shall become one flesh. Therefore, what God joins together, let man not separate" (Berean Literal Bible). Be joined in this passage means to glue or cleave to, in other words, hard to separate (G4347-*proskollao*). The pros and kollao make up the term proskollao. Pros suggest towards, and kollao means to glue. This term is not sexual. It relates to actions and commitment, which can form a covenant. A man and woman vow to *go towards* and *to join* with one another. Another definition says that "someone in a personal (interfacing) relationship, suggesting a more permanent association" (Helps Word-studies). After martial vows, intercourse seals the covenant. (v. 8). However, many other scriptures use the term proskollao, which does not include sexual sin. For instance, 1 Corinthians 6:17 says, but whoever is attached to the Lord is one with Him in spirit (pneuma). Other scriptures with the same reference are Romans 12:9 and Acts 10:28.

Soul ties are like a bridge connecting one person to another, which can be beneficial or destructive. An illegal or unprosperous soul ties welcome devils to the unlawful connection. Furthermore, they use this bridge as a passageway to connect with fornicators or adulterers, especially for tormenting. Fornication is a common bridge, but trauma bonding and co-dependency are other forms of soul ties. Please note that there is a difference between an unlawful soul tie and an unprosperous soul tie. Illegal means a person is forbidden to do or practice. On the other hand, unprosperous means to delay success leading to bondage or dysfunctional cycles.

Sinful or dysfunctional soul ties can fragment the soul causing D.I.D. (dissociative identity disorder). It becomes hard to bond or be joined to another because the soul has an existing connection. On the other hand, divorce, the death of a loved one, and abandonment are examples of existing soul ties that can break or wound the soul for years and even decades. Soul ties thrive on mutuality. However, divorce, death, or abandonment causes the connection to stop abruptly. Mourning helps to comfort a person's soul. It brings relief, and eventually, the grieving person comes to terms with the loss. However, grief must end for the sake of a healthy soul. The Lord said to Joshua, "Moses, my servant is dead. Now arise, you and these people, and cross over the Jordan to the land that I am giving to the children of Israel" (Joshua 1:2). The Lord understands our grief, yet he frees us from death by asking us to lift our eyes to Him (Ps. 121:1-2).

Beneficial soul ties pertain to social or relational relationships, and an example is 1 Samuel 18:1 (KJV). "Moreover, it came to pass when he made an end of speaking unto Saul. The soul of Jonathan was knit with the soul of David. Jonathan loved him as his own soul." In this instance, the nephesh connected and not the pneuma. Unhealthy soul ties lead to obsessions and eventually idolization. Vows and agreements are the terms and conditions that create and bind soul connection. The same is true with vows made with the Lord (Numbers 30:2).

## Abuse of Power and Language

I have found that sarcasm or coarse jesting and anger are the two most dominant traits in abusive people (Ephesians 5:4; Eph 4:29 &30). They find a way to release their anger by putting others down in a crafty unsuspecting way. On the contrary, people who are continually insulted may feel unimportant or mishandled. Sarcasm can trigger people with whom they have soul ties, and this ensures superiority. Sarcasm is rooted in bitterness. Therefore, verbal and emotional abuse follows. It is a tool of empowerment. Therefore, abusive individuals feel emboldened, and their victims feel diminished. More specifically, this is a grooming technique that induces fear. In some cases, victims learn people-pleasing skills to avoid verbal punishment. Inflicting others with verbally abusive speech could trigger an identity crisis. However, taking responsibility for wrongs and dealing with the root of sarcasm is the first step to healing. Taking ownership and working to change can prevent trauma bonding.

Have you ever heard of a hostile work environment? Usually, no signs of physical abuse are found. However, sexual, verbal, emotional, financial, and other abuses of power are. According to a blog, "A hostile environment becomes rewarding and pleasurable only to turn hostile again" (The Cabin. Trauma Bonding, Abusive Relationships, and Addiction). These are the conditions for a trauma bond that involves the brain and dependency.

## Abuse of Power and Trauma Bonding

Trauma bonding is an intense topic, but ultimately it involves the limbic system in the brain. It supports emotions, behavior, long-term memory, and other faculties. Most times, people want to make it past their trauma as quickly as possible. That is why trauma bonding works best in an emotionally abusive relationship. The brain makes connections to everything that aids during a traumatic period—hence being loyal to a fault. However, trauma bonding is not limited to emotional abuse. It can emerge from physical abuse and abduction as well.

Trauma bonding is like a person who plays a dual role. They inflict pain and also ease it away -- that is trauma bonding. One example is the reward after physical abuse. The source of pain is also the source of ease or comfort. Another example could be embarrassing a church member in front of apostles and prophets at a luncheon, then prophesying a grandiose word in a congregation of people about economic wealth and prestige; this is also a form of trauma bonding. Stockholm syndrome is another type of trauma bonding. It is when a victim feels remorse or sympathy for their abuser or captors. Below is a list to help you determine if you have a trauma bond with someone.

- Always worry that you will do something to upset them.
- You go out of your way to protect them.
- You ignore their deviant behavior when others point them out.
- You know they are deceptive and abusive, but you still cannot let go.
- You do everything to please them and are always loyal, even when they give you nothing but pain.
- You hide your emotions from them.
- You feel addicted to them.
- You always have an excuse for them.
- You compromise yourself to please them.
- You forget your worth and value.
- You crave their love and attention.
- You feel you cannot leave, though the situation is toxic for you.
- You feel a relentless need to give the benefit of the doubt.
- You have developed O.C.D. or mimic bipolar disorder.

- Sleeping difficulties or eating problems (too little or too much)
- You doubt yourself and your sanity.
- Easily startled or overactive to everyday situations
- You check your cell phone frequently to see if they called.
- No matter how much you contribute to the relationship, it never seems like enough.
- Experience PTSD or C-PTSD
- You hide their cruelty or abuse and lie to family about your reality.
- You tend to accept accountability for the bad things that happen in your partner's life and feel the need to fix their problems always.
- You do not want to say no or stand up for yourself because you do not want anyone to think you are mean or unwilling to make compromises (Although they are repeatedly mean to you and reluctant to be flexible).
- You rarely go outside the home because there is usually a price to pay, or if you go out, there is always a deep sense of urgency to get back home as quickly as possible.
- You feel invisible. (25 Subtle Signs of Trauma Bonding)

Some of these signs may not apply to you. Nevertheless, if two of these resemble any of your relationships, talk to someone because you may need help. Trauma bonding seriously affects mental processing. Here are a few tips for recovering from trauma bonding. First, live in reality. Making excuses for the other person cannot continue to be your standard. And vice versa. Making excuses for controlling behaviors delays recovery. Grieve for your loss. Your life was linked with another person in ways that merged both of your souls, and that requires grieving. So go through your process of grief. Next is the renunciation phase. You are disconnecting from the other person's toxicity both spiritually, soulish, and emotionally. Renunciation helps to retract vows that legally bind you to the other person. Some call this phase breaking word curses. However, trauma bonding is more than word curses. When souls connect unconventionally, the synergy calls to the other soul even if the person passed away. Two excellent resources about deliverance are "Pigs In The Parlor" by Frank and Ida Mae Hammond and "Deliverance and Spiritual Warfare Manual" by John Eckhardt. Finally, if necessary, connect with a trusted leader, Christian counselor, or therapist.

## Chapter 8 Abuse of Power

Part 2

### Ways to Prevent Trauma Bonding

Remember the term prefrontal cortex. This part of the brain is known as the brain's executive portion. It can help prevent trauma bonding. Below are ways to strengthen the prefrontal cortex.
- Resist instant gratification because it rewires the brain to seek reward immediately.
- Go beyond your comfort zone to make a new neural connection.
- Learn new material.
- Use the best-case scenario idea (optimism)
- Get enough sleep.

- Meditate on God's word and map out how to accomplish the things you would like to change.
- Clean up your diet.

These are important to help the neurotransmitters regulate the fear modulation in the prefrontal cortex. Neurotransmitters have many functions, but for this scenario, I would like to focus on mood. These transmitters concentrate on the action component of the body through signals. Therefore, to improve thinking, intentionally practice behaviors that will enhance good responses. For Christian, this promotes Galatians 6:9 and Matthew 5:16.

The prefrontal cortex connects to the limbic brain (See Photo). Why is this important? Because this proves that everything about our make-up can change and improve, including thoughts. Be renewed in the spirit of your mind can happen (Ephesians 4:23). Think about things that are pure, lovely, commendable, excellent, and worthy of praise is possible by way of the prefrontal cortex.

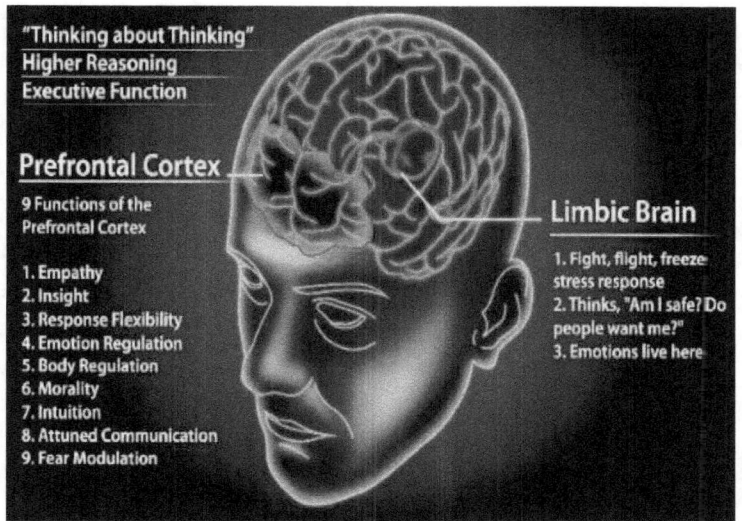

What we think about and what we feel can change. What influences our thinking is another matter. We can change if we intentionally seek help—examine what areas of your life do not match the Lord's standard. Remember, the way a man thinks in his heart, so he is.

## Proof of Identity

Identity theft is a topic that can go on and on. Hopefully, we have covered enough for prophets to recognize the power of abuse, especially concerning codependency and trauma bonding. Now let us talk about proof of identity. God determines when training begins for a prophet. The first portion of training includes elementary basics. Biblically understanding, study habits, disciplines, prayer life, commitment to change, and heart checks. Next comes trials, hardships, and the threshing floor experiences, or the testing stage. It is to test if prophets have altered their behavior rather than changing the way they think. The realms on earth acknowledge and announces the prophet's "coming of age" where on-the-job training happens—finally, the prophet's works and words get backing by heavenly enforcement. In a perfect world, this occurs without interference from the mind and soul. Nevertheless, God starts to cultivate the identity of the prophet at the elementary stages.

Testing and trying their commitment evaluate his or her humility level. The bible says, "The fear of the Lord is instructions of wisdom, and humility comes before honor" (Proverbs 15:33). Vital lessons of integrity are attached to the Lord's teaching. Those teachings are to humble the prophet. The prophet is training for a position, but most importantly, he or she trains to become the embodiment of Christ. As they prepare and go through trials and testing processes, they must choose to stay connected to the Lord. The prophet's new thought processes and behaviors clean out the rubbish of life and any preconditioning. Therefore, God teaches the P.I.T (a prophet in training) how to use power versus abuse it. He shows them the process of humility and honor or succession and predecessor. Abusing power means the prophet emerged too quickly or never finished their grooming process. Identity has a lot to do with who our natural parents are on earth. They play a massive part in genealogy, our view of society, and huge contributors to our core beliefs. However, our true identity is heavenly, and understanding this forges our path through life. Therefore, everything matters and nothing gets wasted (Romans 8:28).

## Other Abuses of Power

Prophets who misappropriate funds are ignorant of something. Hence, neglecting the Proverbs 15:33 model. Where is the wisdom? Governing the donations or income of the Lord is a full-time job. So, the excellence of distribution is not a light matter. Budgets and financial advisors help disseminate resources for the work of the kingdom. Another thing is learning how to command resources. The prophet's mantle attracts economics for the Lord's work and his projects. The prophet has knowledge concerning the production, consumption, and transference of wealth. However, if the prophet remains ignorant concerning finances, they can handicap their sphere of influence, limiting them from their full potential and jamming the flow of heavenly and earthly provisions (2 Corinthians 9:8).

Greed is one of the byproducts of thief and deception. It works with lust to stay deep-rooted in the soul. A greedy prophet will never be content. His or her passion will not be satisfied. One scripture that talks about greed is Ephesian 5:5, "For this, you can be sure: no immoral, impure, or greedy person (that is an idolater) has any inheritance in the kingdom of Christ and God." Greed turns a sanctified person into a dishonorable individual. The greedy person in Ephesians 5:5 is an idolater. Notice that the prophet is now on the wrong side of his or her official duties. Idolatry is treason against the kingdom of Christ and God. How can a prophet double up so quickly?

Next on the list of other abuses is pride. Pride is a word that most people question. Can Godly pride be accepted? Some say that it is confidence, while others say that it shows respect and self-esteem. What do you say? Prophets and believers may not understand how deadly the term pride is. We have listened to the Christian orator's quote Proverbs 16:18. "Pride goes before destruction and a haughty spirit before a fall." However, what does that scripture mean? How can a prophet apply this principle to his/her life?

In context, the term pride in the Strong's concordance, number 1347, is arrogance, majesty, and ornament. Formulated from the Hebrew words ga'ah and ga'avah, which are primitive roots meaning rise. When pride arises, it is to deflect truthfulness. Humanity learns to adapt to mendacity. To change facts to suit the narrative of a proposed plan or hidden agenda. Society dresses pride up as a term of acceptance and liberation, but the expression reveals the wrong fruit.

## Pride Attempts to Hides Things

Pride significantly repels deliverance since it hides or tucks away matters of the heart. Pride conceals truthfulness, which is why haughtiness comes after. Superiority complex makes for a society and culture that is aloof. Remember, fruit is the evidence of what grew over time. The fruit of American culture centers around many things, including covetousness. We blame Wall Street, corporate executives, big lenders, and what can we say about proposed bipartisanship? However, what has greed cost the United States and the American people? These issues come from thoughts and deceit that are decades and even centuries in the making.

I recall 2 Chronicles 34:1-33. This chapter is about a young king named Josiah. He began his reign at the age of eight and had a heart for God. The Bible says that he began to seek the God of David, his father (v.3). Josiah purged Jerusalem and Judah of its idols and altars, then repaired the house of the Lord, and graciously continued to seek God and his counsel. Though Josiah made mistakes, he resisted pride and did not abuse his power. He repelled covetousness, greed, lust, and theft. What took him out was disobedience. None of us are safe from the temptation of sin. However, accountability can help support the load of life.

Josiah did well when he tore down the high places and destroyed the altars of incense. He continued until he purged the false images in the lands that he governed. The wooden gods, the carved images, and the molded images. King Josiah broke in pieces and made dust of them. He scattered *it* on the graves of those who had sacrificed to them, and also burned the priest's bones on their altars, and cleansed Judah and Jerusalem (vv. 4-5). At this point, the king had a limited understanding of God's law. However, while rebuilding the temple, the Book of the Law is found by Hilkiah, the priest (v. 14). King Josiah was not aware of the requirements Yahweh had. Nevertheless, once Shaphan read it to him, he changed. He was humble enough to know that his *works* were right but not enough. Five people were chosen with the task to inquire of the Lord (v. 22). These men went and found Huldah, the prophetess who lived in Jerusalem. Prophetess Huldah had a word from the Lord. She accurately prophesied the future of Israel. Repentance and restoration came because of the righteousness of King Josiah.

Prophets declare the edicts of God, even if the word is not celebratory. Therefore, false honor, false humility, pride, co-dependency, nor trauma bonding should not plague the soul of a prophet. The role of prophets in the American Ecclesia is to purge its custodianship of false images and covetous altars. And to repair the house of the Lord, physically, metaphysically, and interpersonally. Forget about all its *works* and move towards the pure government of Christ. Ekklesia is more than a church meeting. It is a company of Christians that operates as one functional entity. A troop under one director is what the body of Christ represents. People are subject to one another and banded together by the Holy Spirit -- a fully functioning body.

Huldah represents the infallible sound of God, his counsel, and his governmental sanctions. The proof of what humility and a tender heart toward God can bring to a nation is remarkable. A prophet filled with pride is not part of kingdom reformation. King Josiah was a reformer of his time. He led Israel back to God as he partnered with Huldah, the prophetess. Josiah wanted to serve God. So, he put away pride and honored the Lord with his life. Our nation can turn!

Prophet's guide, govern, and guards their area of influence to establish safety and proper people placement for the work of Christ. Manipulation or control frustrates people and the work of the Lord. But prophets help to create safeguards, not fan clubs or people pleasers. Paul said, am I now seeking the favor of men or God? Or am I striving to please men? If I were still trying to please men, I would not be a bondservant of Christ (Galatians 1:10). Guide the souls, guard the gates, and govern your mind, to diligently protect the establishment of Christ, Prophets!

## Chapter 9 Communication Realm

This chapter is for the faithful watchman who prays in and out of season. They are the intercessors, prayer warriors, and prophets who frequently mediate and transport goods from the otherworld, known as the spiritual realm. Intercession is a choice. So, whether it is viewed as a gift or skill, intercession is mediation.

Prophets should take their cues from the chief intercessor, Jesus Christ. He mediates for humanity based on his sovereignty. Romans 8:34 says, Jesus is at the right hand of God – and He is interceding for us. In context, interceding is the word entugchano that comes from two words, en and tygxano. En translates to *in*, as in a place, limits, or space; either abstract or immaterial. On the other hand, tygxano translates to *"obtain by hitting the mark* and *light upon*, (meet with) and converse, consult, and intervene" (HELPS Word-studies).

The term *light upon* properly transposes to intercession because people are enlightened after appropriate prayer. Mainly due to their consultation with the Lord or having spiritual encounters with his angelic beings (Revelations 1:1). Ephesians 1:18-21 says, "I ask that the eyes of your heart be enlightened, so that you may know the hope of His calling, the riches of His glorious inheritance in the saints, and the surpassing greatness of His power to us who believe." Intercessors connect to the heavenly realms through prayer, where a vault of unknowable things becomes knowable, including futuristic events. But the prayer that remains one-dimensional stays in the carnal realm, never bypassing the intercessor's intellect. The definition of intellectualism is the exercise of intelligence at the expense of a person's emotions. It is the seat of conceptualization that leads down many paths. Prayer is a discourse between man and his deity. So, vacillating in one's thoughts while praying is a discussion with oneself, leading to unrealistic projections and self-delusion. An active imagination helps humanity deal with life, enabling us to have a vision of the future. But Christians pray to God for answers and direction. In other religions, prayer and meditation are the same. Therefore, consulting with oneself and centering is the aim. However, measuring prayer in Christianity is necessary to excel past the carnal dimensions into the spirit world. One way to do this is by studying the written word. Another way is by reading Christian books on prayer and intercession.

Books, in general, can open the imaginary dimensions in one's mind, and so can the Holy Scriptures in the Bible. When a reader reads, they automatically imagine the words as pictures. The same is true when we read the Bible. However, we go a step further because scriptures are keys to measure what we believe and where we go in the spiritual world. Scriptures also allow Holy Spirit to navigate through the mental roadblocks that prevent faith in God. Christians, intercessors, and prophets who read and understand the bible either stay in the carnal realm or continue into what I call the school of the Spirit. The Pharisees, Sadducees, scribes, and other religious elects never transcended beyond their religious mindset. They were the ones who remained unenlightened about the basic concept of faith and spiritual works.

*Light up* in intercession is also a part of the glorious light of wisdom or intelligence contained in Christ. He is the reason believers become the light of the world (Matthew 5:14). One scripture says that the Lord lights our darkness as he did for David in Psalm 18:28. Another scripture says that Jesus wanted us to become children of light that do not follow dark ways (John 12:35-36). Essentially, we should become people who bypass the carnal realm. Holy Spirit reveals Christ's mysteries of the unknown when we pray correctly. But what happens when intercessors pray but do not ascend to heavenly realms? They intended to mount to the holy places. However, he or she remained in the realm of the imagination.

The imagination is a peculiar arena where vision is born. A person can create anything by imagining. Their inner vision works on multiple levels and can represent both good and bad, including what is known as an illusion. Calling one's thoughts to the front of the mind is the beginning of conceptualization. As the prayer proceeds, the intercessors envision what they desire at the will of their conscious. There is a difference between praying for what we want and imagining what we want. Then saying, "God showed me a vision in prayer." No, that vision was fueled by their conscious will. At some point, they open the fantasy of their desire versus the revelation of the Lord. The imagination is not evil, but we need vision powered by God through the Holy Spirit. Remember, we are who Christ is only if we walk in the light as little children (John 12:35-36). Children follow because they are trusting in nature, and adults keep them safe from dangerous predators. The same is true about the imaginary realms; vanity, idolatry, and other evil desires form there. So we need Christ's protection and guidance. One scripture says, "People became vain in their imagination, and their foolish hearts became darkened (Romans 1:21). Another scripture says, "Do not to listen to the prophets who fill you with false hope and speak visions from their vain imagination or mind" (Jer. 23:16). Our job is to pray with the intent of petition and fellowship. These two categories encompass many prayer themes.

Prophets connect in prayer to stay aligned to the will of Yahweh, not because they cannot network without Him, but true prophets want to remain connected to their source; this ensures their authenticity to the truth of the word. A relational connection is just as crucial as a professional connection. If a prophet connects for relationship and officiality, their love, honor, and commitment to Yahweh will develop.

Ephesians 1:18 and 19 says, "I pray that the eyes of your heart may be enlightened so that you may know the hope in which he has called you, the riches of his glorious inheritance in his holy people, and his incomparably great power for us who believe. That power is the same as mighty strength." Three factors are revealed in Ephesians 1:18-19, to know the hope of His calling, to know the riches of God's inheritance in the saints, and to know the greatness of God's power. Ignorance is the first thing that Yahweh addresses in this scripture. Most people ask questions like, why am I here? Knowing the hope of God's calling relates to the expectation that believers will understand their vocation. The prophet has a choice to know and then demonstrate God's hope and calling and address issues that oppose His kingdom mandate. This occupation comes with multiple job requirements, especially prayer. Next, the scriptures address discovering and possessing the riches awarded to the saint (set-apart ones). These are believers who are fundamentally different because of sonship; the bible calls them saints.

Saint comes from the Greek word *hagios*, which means different, unlike, and otherness. It also means the likeness of the Lord's nature, and technically they are different from the world because they "like the Lord" (HELPS Word-studies). Saints are qualified beneficiaries of the promises Christ gave to the Christian believer. Finally, the scripture says to know the transcending greatness of His power. We learn the excellence of power by frequent visitations into the presence of the Lord. After we reposition ourselves to the will of the Lord, then we encounter the miraculous power, might, and strength of Yahweh in prayer. Touching his power source of Supremacy in prayer activates the prophet to conduit God's power. Yes, proper prayer initiates *Dunamis*.

Prayer is the precursor to transcending into intercession and mediation. Furthermore, knowing the genuine power, might, and strength of the Lord helps intercessors and prophets differentiate between false visions or signs from demonic influences and true pure Dunamis from God. Powerlessness might be a sign of relational deficiency with Christ. Or their perception of the Lord is that he serves them like a *genie*. God becomes real to the prophet in prayer, and there are no disguises between the Lord and His people. He recognizes his prophets, and his prophets know Him as well.

Prophets intercede to model the character and behavior of Christ. Before Christ's resurrection, he continually stole away to pray. The helps Word-studies puts it to *go* and *meet* to *consult* and *converse*. Jesus understood the relational connection concept, and it fueled his passion for the cross. Each prophet has an intercessory assignment that creates pure traction in the spirit world. However, a prayerless prophet cannot be trusted. The source of their knowledge can be faulty even if he or she is accurate. Prophets meet and converse with God because of their relationship.

The makeup of a prophet outfits him or her to have connections without training. Some prophets remember dreaming of future events when they were children. Some saw in the spiritual realms. Many suppressed or rationalized their gifts to avoid scrutiny and mental institutions. However, prayer can help prophets sustain a whole and healthy soul through communion with Elohim. He restores our soul is not a bedtime prayer. It is a foundational key for a whole life. Jesus understood the sensitivity and fragileness of his soul. So, he fought to protect it through convening with Adonai. Another definition of intercession means to obtain by hitting the mark. When we pray accurately, we receive what we asked for in prayer.

Prophets are like attorneys, but they start as a type of legal assistant. They learn the spiritual terrains, gather information, and study with a mentor to help with development. Some prophets start as intercessors. Eventually, they grow into higher graces of prayer. He or she nurtures their passion for mediation and prays for others continuously. Healthy intercession includes balance and accountability but, unhealthy mediation can lead to obsessive and controlling behaviors. The downside of intercession is a false burden. False burdens can wound prophetic intercessors as they take on tasks outside of their sphere or assignments. How many times have intercessors taken on other people's warfare because they were outside their sphere of rule (2 Corinthians 10:13)? Please keep in mind that everything is not your assignment. This premise will help alleviate false burdens. When in doubt, accountability is a great balancer.

## Communication: Actions and Behaviors

Prophets hear audibly. Usually, he or she hears in their thoughts or heart. Divine communication gives prophets access to the spiritual graces that activate new dimensions. When this happens, the prophet becomes a steward of the revealed dimension.

Communication is also actions and behaviors. When a minister lays their hand on someone while they pray, this is a point of contact. Communication creates openness. Our receptiveness to God creates waves that travel back and forth from our inner man or spirit man to the Sovereign-God in prayer. Though we think about communication as networking, we are exchanging data in the same space. One misconception that I would like to address is where God is. John 14:23 says, "He said, if anyone loves me, my Father will love him. We will come to Him and make our home with

Him." Jesus tells us that the prerequisite for his indwelling in us is love. Officially God is in heaven. However, he is omnipresent and can dwell wherever welcomed.

Most Prophets understand communication with God, not from the premise of distance because most prophets hear internally. Prophetic words form from our spirit, not from the soul. What we transmit to God and what He speaks back happens in the spirit world. Think of it as being in the same place but in a different dimension. The spirit world is a realm with a modified system. It operates based on specific regulations like the earth. Physicality or earthly material cannot exist in that realm. Therefore, the inward man connects to the spirit world through prayer and, more specifically, by words and faith. Therefore, God's conversation with believers and prophets happens in our inward part where he dwells.

The false or pseudo prophet also connects to the spirit world. They communicate with the spirit world through their spirit man and use dark art and intellect to persuade the hearer. The imagination is the most excellent tool of deceit. Matthew 24:24 says, "For false Christ, and false prophets will rise and show great signs and wonders to deceive, if possible, even the elect." In Strong's Exhaustive Concordance number 5578, the false prophet is two words pseudes and prophetes: pseudes means false, deceitful, lying, untrue; prophetes means an interpreter or forth-teller of the divine will. The Helps Word-studies explains prophetes as pro (4253) "beforehand" and phemi (5346), "elevating or asserting one idea over another, especially through the spoken word. One who speaks forth by the inspiration of God; a prophet. A prophet declares the mind (message) of God, which sometimes predicts the future (foretelling) – and more commonly, speak forth His message of a particular situation."

"A prophet is someone inspired by God to foretell or tell-forth the Word of God" (Helps Ministries, Inc.) A spurious prophet is the opposite expression of a true prophet. He or she is a pretender and religious imposter, known as a false prophet. Any communication that leads people away from Christ is pseudo.

### Communication: Worship Posture

Worship is a commonly used phrase, and though we touched it in the previous chapter, we revisit it here as a communication tool. Worship prescribed by man fails, but worship prescribed by God brings glory. Worship is two words, *pros*, and *kyneo* (Strong's number 4352). It means to do reverence, to go towards, and to kiss (John 423). Glory is the aftermath of presence, and God's presence comes through intimacy. Finally, intimacy is the byproduct of communication. Therefore, proper and appropriate worship is genuine.

Revelation 19:10 says, "And I fell at his feet to worship him. And he said to me, See thou do it not: I am your fellow servant, and of your brethren who have the testimony of Jesus: Worship God! For the testimony of Jesus is the Spirit of prophecy." True prophets testify of Jesus, and most importantly, he or she resembles Him as well. Worship is an action. Nevertheless, people worship because of what they know. Prayer helps us understand God's person. We learn his motives, attributes, patterns, and personality traits. Like with a parent who has adult kids, disrespect is not an option. However, conversations are different, and trust remains based on interpersonal relationships. The kids have no reason to prove a connection or relationship to their parents because the fruit of their relationship shows naturally and vice versa.

Prophets who need to prove something to others worry me, primarily due to unauthentic manifestations. They need recognition and approval and are willing to do anything to be relevant, so ambitions drive their motivations and actions. The Bible says, "Woe to the foolish prophets, who follow their spirit and have seen nothing" (Ezekiel 13:3). Lack of communication causes a lack of worship. Seemingly, connection to false sources can damage a prophet's perception and cause presumption. Biblical-based prayer weeds out the faulty connection and slowly changes the heart, which changes the prophet's worship posture and source of worship. Ambition cannot be why prophets prophesy. It disqualifies him or her from the original fold of authentic prophets of the Lord (Deuteronomy 18:20). Prophets must take time for personal prayer as well. It builds foundational faith that creates healthy intercessors.

As a prophet grows, his or her word life should grow as well. Soon after, God will start the process of deflation. He begins by revealing the personality traits in the prophet that fights against his voice and character. There are a couple of stages the trainee goes through. They learn how to connect with the Spirit of God correctly. Sometimes, this lesson takes years. The next training is all about faith. A faith-filled prophet believes in prayer and establishes a profound bond with the Holy Spirit. Next comes the lessons of humility and soundness. A prophet's mental health is their greatest weapon against falsehoods. These lessons are essential to a balanced intercessor and prophet.

### The Mechanics of Prayer

When intercessors pray, their spirit-man attune to signals known as frequency. The same is true with prophets. Intercessors frequently link to the spiritual world by authorizing their spirit-man to be in constant communication with God through prayer. They can most often be mistaken for a prophet because of their strong traction in prayer. It is what privy's them to access the spirit world's information. Ascending into the spirit realm is a familiar road for intercessors. However, the danger is the weightiest of their experiences there. I have witnessed unsettling occurrences in prayer gatherings, and the most terrifying is hearing what people say they saw and experienced with "*God.*" Most are in the imaginary or sensory realms rather than the otherworldly. The imaginary realm is real. So intercessors and prophets should be accountable. Mature, senior, or chief prophets can help prophetic intercessory agents navigate past imagination. Sobriety is a prophet's best defense against falsehoods and impure connections. Prophets who learn foundational lessons have a sound basis for all visitations, dreams, visions, experiences, and information acquired in the spirit world. Some of the pseudo manifestations of false prophetic are below (Naim Collins, Realms of the Prophetic, pg.206-208):

- Twisted teaching to draw people to themselves (Acts 20:30)
- They follow their spirit.
- Deceitful and lying signs and wonders (Matthew 21:24)
- Foolish, lying, silly, goofy prophet (Ezekiel 13:3-7)
- Delusive vision (Ezekiel 13:3-7)
- Divination (false prophetic spirit), clairvoyance, witches, warlock, mediums, psychics, palm and tarot card readers, ESP, etc. (Ezekiel 13:3-7)
- Soulish, carnal, and fleshy prophets (Ezekiel 13:3-7)
- False prophets receive inspiration from demons (Ezekiel 13:3-7)

Finally, an unclean nature is another sign of a pseudo prophet. Fornication, idolatry, adultery, etc., break connection and communication with Yahweh. What these prophets manifest is their gift but not from the office. Officials are representatives of their Sovereign, not of themselves. Therefore, chastity is not an option. It is a lifestyle and a choice. Prophet who sleeps around, flirt, lie, deceive, control others, manipulate, lust for money, compete with others, hold grudges, envy, or are jealous are inappropriate representatives of the Lord. And they compromise themselves, others, and their mission.

## Chapter 10 Glory Carriers

Glory Carriers exist across the globe. They carry the substance and essence of God's infinite, intrinsic worth. We represent the word Doxa. One author said that Doxa is a 'perfect inward part or personal excellence of Christ using 2 Cor. 3:18 as his premise. Doxa also relates to the exterior brightness that beams from beings, including angels. It reminds me of the glory that Christians put on, like a "cloak of glory" called *addereth* (Strong's 155). More specifically, the cloak of a prophetic mantle is found in 1 Kings 19:13,19 and 2 Kings 2:8,13 & 14. Addyir is a hairy garment in Genesis 25:25. Nonetheless, it comes from two words, addyir and eder. Addyir means something ample, and eder means glory, garment, goodly, mantle, and robe. Glory Carriers retain something marvelous based on what is within and what is without. There are other qualities and benefits of carrying God's glory as well. Nevertheless, there is nothing that we can take credit for because our glory reflects His excellency.

Doxa also represents honor, praise, respect, gratitude, and other things. Shakina is another word for glory. It means to dwell or settle in a place. Kabod is yet another word for glory found in scriptures. The kabod is the weight or the heaviness of the Lord, and it contains eternity. Not only is the Kabod all the things previously mentioned, but it also includes abundant riches, the dignity of position, honor, splendor, and glory of external conditions and circumstance. Our Sovereign is looking for people who will be filled with his glory. These are kingdom citizens who know their God. Honor and praise precede the dwelling and settling of the Lord. Afterward, the weight and the presence of the Lord unlock our understanding of how to carry God's glory. All of this brings us to the scripture that says, "The kingdom of God is in you" (Luke 17:21). The glory of God is in the kingdom of God.

For note-takers, below are other Hebrew and Greek words for the term of glory:
- yeqar (H3367)
- hadar (H1926)
- hod (H1935)
- kauchema (G2745)
- kabod (H3519)
- Ploutos (G4149)

During the coronavirus pandemic, I got sick. The first few days, I had spiritual encounters, and I dreamed many things. I did not know about the pandemic, and I did not foresee the presidential election. However, God allowed me to see what was prevalent to my vocation and sphere. Before this, I underwent a series of new training. Number one, God needed me to understand his glory. My primary training included understanding my assignment as a Glory Carrier, not in theory but as a premise for life. Training people about spiritual things is the second thing that God revealed about my calling. Therefore, the training was for a kingdom cause. Towards the end of that season, the Lord spoke to me several times about spiritually training others, but I did not move. However, when he gave me the outline for what he wanted me to build, I began to pray. After almost a year of incubation and gestation (prayer, research, and waiting on God's timetabling). He said, pay attention to who I send to you. It started with people from a local college, and afterward, they were finding me from different parts of the US.

So, I started the Glory Carriers Co back in 2016 because it was time. Today, we have grown into a community that trains in the prophetic, deliverance, soul healing, foundational biblical studies, and so much more. Our focal areas are transparency and honesty because transparency helps in the healing process, and honesty forges trust. One prerequisite for this is "Truth in the inward parts" (Ps. 51:6). Being honest allows us to practice self-awareness.

On August 15, 2019, I wrote a blog in the Glory Carriers Facebook Group entitled Pellucid Ones. The purpose was to express who glory carriers are and why God wanted them. It reads:

*I am grateful to have all of you as participants of Glory Carriers Spiritual Training Group. We are less than one month away from our first anniversary, and I am super excited. Part of me is overwhelmed at how God brings clarity about who we are and why He created us. God is truly clear about what he expects from us as a nation. The question is, "Are we clear"?*

*The word clarity mentioned previously means free from darkness, without cloudiness or pellucid. We are His pellucid ones! We allow the maximum passage of light (like glass) to pass through us and fill us, hence transforming us into Glory Carriers! We are the light of the world, and the light that illuminates from us has a source. Jesus said, "I am the light of the world. Whoever follows me will never walk in darkness but will have the light of life" (John 6:51 emphasis added).*

*The more we live in Christ, the more we embrace His truth of who we are. Truth and light run together, I imagine, like twin horses. And their purpose is to expose the darkness. This includes our underdeveloped places (mind, heart, will, disciplines, words, emotions, etc.). Light uncovers, reveals, exposes, and heals. Jesus cannot hide light (Matthew 5:14)! The very nature of light is to radiate. Its function is to extend or disseminate itself until it can go no further. If this is true - we, therefore, cannot be hidden. We, therefore, cannot be stopped. We, therefore, are to extend God's kingdom, sowing seed everywhere He's called us to, and to promulgate who we shine for.*

*I am reminded of the beautiful text which says, "They that know their God shall prove themselves strong and shall stand firm and do exploits for Him (Daniel 11:32 Amplified Classic Edition). What makes us strong has nothing to do with physical strength, knowledge, or even power. Our strength comes from the ultimate source of power - The Sovereign One. He is the one whom authors record as, "Yours, Lord, is the greatness and the power and the Glory and the majesty and the splendor, for everything in heaven and earth is yours. Yours, Lord, is the kingdom; you are exalted as head overall." 1 Chronicle 29:11. And what about, "Ah, Sovereign Lord, you have made the heavens and the earth by your great power and outstretched arm. Nothing is too hard for you." Jeremiah 32:17.*

*These scriptures reflect not only the power of God but also his authorship. To say the least of Him would be robbery. God is our Glory! Without him, we live to please ourselves as false authors of life. Today, I am grateful to you for your commitment to Christ and your commitment to learn, grow, and transform, which is our purpose statement. My prayer is that you continue to become all God created you to be. Not what man has limited you to see concerning who you are, what you are, and why He says you should continue to exist. If you have not already, claim your right as a Glory Carrier and live for Christ and His kingdom."*

I wrote this letter as an encouragement to the Glory Carriers Spiritual Training and Mentorship group members. For many reading this, you have already become aware of your prophetic bent. You can see, hear, discern, and peer into the spirit world. Knowing these secrets and mysteries either overwhelmed you or intrigued you. These times are very crucial because your newfound skills will determine whom your heart will serve. Sadly, some prophets become loyal to the people in charge of a ministry or church. Valid Glory Carriers are committed to Yahweh-God first, not to a man or selfish ambition. Nevertheless, the ministerial assignment causes us to be loyal to the body of believers as well.

Glory Carriers are not a perfectionist. They make mistakes and repent. Furthermore, when they are in transition, they focus on the leading of Abba more intently. The perfectionist model ends with God's Glory Carriers, and the model of competency, skill, and commitment begins. The mandate of love, joy, kindness, and other fruit helps us resemble Christ and draw other believers to the God-first appointment. God cares much about how we act and what we do. Therefore, Godly representation is everything to the Lord. How we behave categorizes who we are and who fathers us (John 8:44). Glory Carriers are not crude, evil, controlling, or misrepresentations of Yahweh. They embrace the most excellent gift called love. It does not suggest that Glory Carriers do not become angry or do not have arguments, but they do not sin when these emotions arise. Glory Carriers are in society, as local nurses, attorneys, teachers, hygienists, CEOs, students, psychologists, business owners, foster parents, baristas, janitors, entrepreneurs, CPAs, cashiers, and other professionals. They are not ignorant of societal involvement, and they extend themselves outside of the church walls. Their identity is not only connected to their 5-fold status. Their identity reflects balanced connections and relationships, especially with the Lord.

### New Era Where People Are In Training

I posted another letter in the group while we were on a community fast. A portion of the letter is below.

*"We are at the beginning of something new. There is a new opening that recently came into existence with a fixed timeframe. It is to begin a series that humanity and this planet have never seen before. God is sending out warnings. Watch your connections! Fix your connections! The enemy is looking to sever and disconnect good (God) connections.*

*We are a new era of people in training, and God will show us how to have visual celibacy. Visual celibacy is choosing to vet everything before it is viewed or accepted, including books, magazines, sitcoms, memes, shows, movies, social media lives, and posts. Do not become contaminated by the things that the world throws at you. The false perception of perfection is here. God said, "I'm stripping off the mask of perfection." God is calling us up to a new plane and new training. Prophets arise and get trained! The new era assignment is not about the people you want to save, but about people God called you to help save.*

Again, Yahweh-God allowed me to hear, see, discern, and prepare the letter based on my sphere of influence. I shared what the Lord showed me with the GC community because He said so. Afterward, I designed a new course called Soul 101 on an online platform for the Glory Carriers Community. Up until that time, I had a rough draft of this book with no significant leeway, but I used what I had to create an online e-book for the course. The Spirit of the Lord instructed me on the course material and even what to charge. When we reached the third class, God expanded my knowledge through our relational connection. His words changed me and my sphere of influence.

Prophets are one of the deliverance tools that God uses outside of prophesying. Our ability to see into God's heart and thoughts should press us beyond where we are societally, spiritually, and professionally. However, that is not always the case. In this new era, the old way of thinking, living, and doing things will change because we are changing. Here are some last thoughts about God's words regarding the Coronavirus. It is what He called the neuropathic disruptors. I had a prophetic dream while I was ill. In the dream realm, a female prophet came to me and gave me a piece of paper with neuropathic disruptors written on it. I said, "Lord, you know I do not know anything about biology." The exciting thing is, I didn't say that out loud. I said it as the dreamer, but not as the character in the dream. The female prophet in my dream walked away, and I woke up. As soon as I woke up, I was on high response alert. First, I jotted down my experience. Then I asked the Lord to give me wisdom about the dream. It was not long after, and he reminded me of a trip that I took to Alpharetta, Georgia. At the meeting, the hosting apostle said that God said legions are behind a coming sickness. He also said, 'there is a sickness called Legionnaires disease that affects the lungs.' Until now, I forgot that word and the 2018 trip. When the memory was over, the Spirit of God said, find legions. I looked at the story in several translations and different books of the Bible. But I was stumped. What did God want me to know? I looked up neuropathic disruptors. When I did, I found topics like neuropathic pain, endocrine disruptors, nerve disruptors. However, nothing was like the words in the note in my dream.

Finally, I prayed for the Lord to let me see what He needed me to see. He showed me the condition of the man in Matthew 8, Mark 5, and Luke 8. The plagued of evil spirits created a system that dominated the total man. However, I also saw something interesting in Matthew 26:53, twelve legions of angels, another representation of a systematic force. At that moment, I understood that the Lord would disrupt the systems. Jesus disrupted the system in the city of Gerasene and in the man tormented with the legion. A system thrives based on what is allowed in an environment (2 Thessalonian 2:7). The earth's inhabitants collectively conceded to sins that caused a global network to emerge, sound familiar (Noah and the flood). It does not matter whether people created Coronavirus in a lab or not. It is a well-organized system that affects the body in ways that causes sickness and death.

In my research, I found that neuropathy is any diseased condition affecting the nervous system and its transmission of signals to different parts of the body becomes inhibited. On a physical level, an intact appropriately functioning nervous system is critical for all human endeavors. It exerts unconscious control over essential body functions, such as respiration, temperature regulations, and movement coordination (Lippincott, Williams and Wilkins, pg.682). The nervous system consists of the central nervous system and the peripheral system. One system controls the brain and spinal cord, while the other consists of nerves that branch off from the spinal cord, known as the cranial spinal and peripheral nerves (National Institutes of Health). It controls the mechanics neurologically, which includes glia, neurons, and nerves. God created the body to run well, and disruptors obstruct that process.

However, neuropathy is damage or dysfunction. Neuropathy is related to pain and degenerative or deterioration caused by injury, infection, disease, drugs, toxins, or vitamin deficiency. The suffix *ic* means pertaining to or denoting of the prefix. Therefore, neuropathic explains neuropathy. Neuropathy is defined by Merriam-Webster dictionary as: an individual subject to nervous disorders or neuroses.

Neuropathic Disruptors prove to be a corrective measure. God's disruptors add a reset to a compromised environment. Disrupting the programing of the adverse effects in the nervous system ensures restoration in the body. No more miss fires or irregularities. What was once diseased, in pain, non-operational, or infected take a turn towards health and wellness.

All in all, God spoke unconventionally about two parts of the body that maintain human existence: the brain and the skeleton. If the brain cannot talk to the body, the body becomes inhibited in many ways. In as much, if God cannot communicate with his body (Ekklesia), then the same dysfunction of the natural neurological defects affects us. Is God's body inhibited? God's messaging is clear about disrupting what is corrupted.

Therefore, I encourage you to look at where you are and decide what matters the most. Move into action the way the Lord leads you. Some will return to the educational institutions. For others, you will connect with people to expand your mental, physical, and relational connections. Others of you will be looking into your health care and readjusting your diet. No matter what your changes look like, remember that you can accomplish anything if you gather information. Welcome to your new assignment, Glory Carrier!

**Disclaimer I am not a doctor, medical professional, or neurologist. Please use this information at your discretion. **

**The END**

## ABOUT THE AUTHOR

Judith John is the CEO and Founder of Glory Carriers CO, JJ Soul Sessions & Looking Glass Developmental Center. Judith John is a mother, mentor, prophet, and Biblical Cognitive Behavioral Therapist professional based in South Florida. From immigrant parents, her story consists of failures, lessons, and triumphs.

Judith John uses her platform and expertise to assist clients with soul healing. Her clientele ranges from young adults to professionals. She guides them toward reconciling their past and uses Biblical cognitive behavioral therapy as her method of choice.

As a mentor, she aids people with step-by-step coaching that aids them towards a promising future by setting goals and creating activities focused on the importance of self-awareness and productivity to enhance success toward their short-term aims. Clients learn how to prepare for their future while resolving unhelpful patterns and behaviors related to the past.

Judith also works with young adults and young people through the Looking Glass Development Center. Students overcoming anxiety can find beneficial activities. Looking Glass provides a space for the creatives at heart. Participants learn about self-awareness, focus strategies, and so much more. Participants have opportunities to express joy, love, and other emotions through dance, spoken word, poetry, or music. Looking Glass Academy is Judith's newest endeavor. This program walks participants through twelve weeks of financial, relational, and other essential skills necessary for everyday success.

Judith enjoys being a mother of four with four beautiful godchildren, loving and raising them to fulfill their greatest potentials.

You can find Judith John on social media platforms.
Instagram: @glorycarriersco @lookingglassDEL
Facebook: #jjsoulsessions (Facebook Group is by invitation only)
Websites:
www.glorycarriersco.com
www.lookingglassdevelopmentctr.com

# Citations

Bible Hub. (2020, December 23) Matthew 10:28. Retrieved from Strong's Greek: 4983. σῶμα (sóma) -- a body (biblehub.com)

Med Circle. (2020, February 26). What Are The 4 Types Of OCD? Retrieved from https://medcircle.com/articles/what-are-the-4-types-of-ocd/

Dictionary.com. Oppression. Retrieved from https://www.dictionary.com/browse/oppression?s=t

Eph. 1:19 (saints - 40. Hagios). Retrieved from https://biblehub.com/greek/40.htm

Ephesian 1:19 (power – 1411. Dunamis). Retrieved from https://biblehub.com/greek/1411.htm

Romans 8:34 (Interceding - 1793. Entugchano). Retrieved from https://biblehub.com/greek/1793.htm

Pelion. Retrieved from https://biblehub.com/greek/4119.htm

Echo. Retrieved from https://biblehub.com/greek/2192.htm

Medical News Today, Codependency (2017, October 31). Retrieved from https://www.medicalnewstoday.com/articles/319873#treatment-for-codependency

The Cabin. (2014, November 6). Codependency and Addiction: Symptoms and Treatments. Retrieved from https://www.thecabinchiangmai.com/blog/infosheet/codependency-and-addiction-symptoms-and-treatment/#:~:text=People%20who%20have%20codependent%20behaviours%20often%20have%20the,feelings.%205%20Poor%20communication%20skills.%20More%20items...%20

YouTube. (2020, January 22). Seven Ways You Can Strengthen Pre-Frontal Cortex. Retrieved from https://www.youtube.com/watch?v=AK8aZJHKX9o&feature=emb_logo

Abuse warrior. 25 Subtle Signs of Trauma Bonding. Retrieved from https://abusewarrior.com/toxic-relationships/narcissistic-abuse/signs-of-trauma-bonding/

Neuroscience of Dating Picture. Retrieved from https://neuroscienceofdating.com/wp-content/uploads/2017/01/300-dpi-prefrontal-cortex-vs-limbic-CHART.CROPPED.jpg

Dictionary.com. Neuropathy. Retrieved from https://www.dictionary.com/browse/neuropathic?s=t

National Institute of Health. (2018, October 10). Retrieved from https://www.nichd.nih.gov/health/topics/neuro/conditioninfo/parts

Jensen, Sharon. *Nursing Health Assessment: A Best Practice Approach.* Wolter Kluwer Health/ Lippincott Williams & Wilkins Philadelphia, PA 2011

Merriam-Webster. (1828). Neuropathy. Retrieved from https://www.merriam-webster.com/dictionary/neuropathy

The Free Dictionary. Farlex, Inc. Retrieved from https://medical-dictionary.thefreedictionary.com/-ical

Healthline. What's an Identity Crisis, and Could You Be Having One? Retrieved from Identity Crisis: Definition, Symptoms, Causes, and Treatment (healthline.com)

www.ingramcontent.com/pod-product-compliance
Lightning Source LLC
Chambersburg PA
CBHW070303010526
44108CB00039B/1664